Data Cleaning

A Practical Perspective

Synthesis Lectures on Data Management

Editor
M. Tamer Özsu, *University of Waterloo*

Synthesis Lectures on Data Management is edited by Tamer Özsu of the University of Waterloo. The series will publish 50- to 125 page publications on topics pertaining to data management. The scope will largely follow the purview of premier information and computer science conferences, such as ACM SIGMOD, VLDB, ICDE, PODS, ICDT, and ACM KDD. Potential topics include, but not are limited to: query languages, database system architectures, transaction management, data warehousing, XML and databases, data stream systems, wide scale data distribution, multimedia data management, data mining, and related subjects.

Data Cleaning: A Practical Perspective
Venkatesh Ganti and Anish Das Sarma
2013

Data Processing on FPGAs
Jens Teubner and Louis Woods
2013

Perspectives on Business Intelligence
Raymond T. Ng, Patricia C. Arocena, Denilson Barbosa, Giuseppe Carenini, Luiz Gomes, Jr. Stephan Jou, Rock Anthony Leung, Evangelos Milios, Renée J. Miller, John Mylopoulos, Rachel A. Pottinger, Frank Tompa, and Eric Yu
2013

Semantics Empowered Web 3.0: Managing Enterprise, Social, Sensor, and Cloud-based Data and Services for Advanced Applications
Amit Sheth and Krishnaprasad Thirunarayan
2012

Data Management in the Cloud: Challenges and Opportunities
Divyakant Agrawal, Sudipto Das, and Amr El Abbadi
2012

Query Processing over Uncertain Databases
Lei Chen and Xiang Lian
2012

Foundations of Data Quality Management
Wenfei Fan and Floris Geerts
2012

Incomplete Data and Data Dependencies in Relational Databases
Sergio Greco, Cristian Molinaro, and Francesca Spezzano
2012

Business Processes: A Database Perspective
Daniel Deutch and Tova Milo
2012

Data Protection from Insider Threats
Elisa Bertino
2012

Deep Web Query Interface Understanding and Integration
Eduard C. Dragut, Weiyi Meng, and Clement T. Yu
2012

P2P Techniques for Decentralized Applications
Esther Pacitti, Reza Akbarinia, and Manal El-Dick
2012

Query Answer Authentication
HweeHwa Pang and Kian-Lee Tan
2012

Declarative Networking
Boon Thau Loo and Wenchao Zhou
2012

Full-Text (Substring) Indexes in External Memory
Marina Barsky, Ulrike Stege, and Alex Thomo
2011

Spatial Data Management
Nikos Mamoulis
2011

Database Repairing and Consistent Query Answering
Leopoldo Bertossi
2011

Managing Event Information: Modeling, Retrieval, and Applications
Amarnath Gupta and Ramesh Jain
2011

Fundamentals of Physical Design and Query Compilation
David Toman and Grant Weddell
2011

Methods for Mining and Summarizing Text Conversations
Giuseppe Carenini, Gabriel Murray, and Raymond Ng
2011

Probabilistic Databases
Dan Suciu, Dan Olteanu, Christopher Ré, and Christoph Koch
2011

Peer-to-Peer Data Management
Karl Aberer
2011

Probabilistic Ranking Techniques in Relational Databases
Ihab F. Ilyas and Mohamed A. Soliman
2011

Uncertain Schema Matching
Avigdor Gal
2011

Fundamentals of Object Databases: Object-Oriented and Object-Relational Design
Suzanne W. Dietrich and Susan D. Urban
2010

Advanced Metasearch Engine Technology
Weiyi Meng and Clement T. Yu
2010

Web Page Recommendation Models: Theory and Algorithms
Sule Gündüz-Ögüdücü
2010

Multidimensional Databases and Data Warehousing
Christian S. Jensen, Torben Bach Pedersen, and Christian Thomsen
2010

Database Replication
Bettina Kemme, Ricardo Jimenez-Peris, and Marta Patino-Martinez
2010

Relational and XML Data Exchange
Marcelo Arenas, Pablo Barcelo, Leonid Libkin, and Filip Murlak
2010

User-Centered Data Management
Tiziana Catarci, Alan Dix, Stephen Kimani, and Giuseppe Santucci
2010

Data Stream Management
Lukasz Golab and M. Tamer Özsu
2010

Access Control in Data Management Systems
Elena Ferrari
2010

An Introduction to Duplicate Detection
Felix Naumann and Melanie Herschel
2010

Privacy-Preserving Data Publishing: An Overview
Raymond Chi-Wing Wong and Ada Wai-Chee Fu
2010

Keyword Search in Databases
Jeffrey Xu Yu, Lu Qin, and Lijun Chang
2009

Data Cleaning: A Practical Perspective
Venkatesh Ganti and Anish Das Sarma

ISBN: 978-3-031-00769-9 paperback
ISBN: 978-3-031-01897-8 ebook

DOI 10.1007/978-3-031-01897-8

A Publication in the Springer series
SYNTHESIS LECTURES ON DATA MANAGEMENT

Lecture #36
Series Editor: M. Tamer Özsu, *University of Waterloo*
Series ISSN
Synthesis Lectures on Data Management
Print 2153-5418 Electronic 2153-5426

Data Cleaning

A Practical Perspective

Venkatesh Ganti
Alation Inc.

Anish Das Sarma
Google Inc.

SYNTHESIS LECTURES ON DATA MANAGEMENT #36

ABSTRACT

Data warehouses consolidate various activities of a business and often form the backbone for generating reports that support important business decisions. Errors in data tend to creep in for a variety of reasons. Some of these reasons include errors during input data collection and errors while merging data collected independently across different databases. These errors in data warehouses often result in erroneous upstream reports, and could impact business decisions negatively. Therefore, one of the critical challenges while maintaining large data warehouses is that of ensuring the quality of data in the data warehouse remains high. The process of maintaining high data quality is commonly referred to as *data cleaning*.

In this book, we first discuss the goals of data cleaning. Often, the goals of data cleaning are not well defined and could mean different solutions in different scenarios. Toward clarifying these goals, we abstract out a common set of data cleaning tasks that often need to be addressed. This abstraction allows us to develop solutions for these common data cleaning tasks. We then discuss a few popular approaches for developing such solutions. In particular, we focus on an operator-centric approach for developing a data cleaning platform. The operator-centric approach involves the development of customizable operators that could be used as building blocks for developing common solutions. This is similar to the approach of relational algebra for query processing. The basic set of operators can be put together to build complex queries. Finally, we discuss the development of custom scripts which leverage the basic data cleaning operators along with relational operators to implement effective solutions for data cleaning tasks.

KEYWORDS

data cleaning, deduplication, record matching, data cleaning scripts, schema matching, ETL, clustering, record matching, deduplication, data standardization, ETL data flows, set similarity join, segmentation, parsing, string similarity functions, edit distance, edit similarity, jaccard similarity, cosine similarity, soundex, constrained deduplication, blocking

Contents

Preface

Data cleaning is the process of starting with raw data from one or more sources and maintaining reliable quality for your applications. We were motivated to write this book since we found a gap in technical material that clearly explained the goals and capabilities of a data cleaning solution; in general, data cleaning is usually thought of as a solution for an individual problem. One of the prominent issues we had was that there was no guide offering practical advice on options available for building or choosing a data cleaning solution. In this book, we fill this gap.

Our approach toward this book was to conceptualize data cleaning solutions as being composed of *tasks* and *operators*. Each solution is a composition of multiple high-level tasks, and each task may have one or more operator-based solutions. In this book we elaborate on the most common tasks, and their implementations leveraging critical operators. Our book can be seen as a practitioner's guide to understand the space of options for evaluating or building a good data cleaning solution. We provide an overview of the capabilities required in such a system, which are the set of tasks described in this book. People building complete solutions may use the set of tasks described here, and choose from the space of operators. Therefore, this book is ideally suited for practitioners of data cleaning and students interested in the topic. Although our book lists the useful tools, techniques, and pointers, some of them require custom implementations with no open-source components available. Therefore, if students or engineers are looking for good abstractions for plugins to build, we hope that our book provides some options.

For beginners interested in data cleaning, we suggest reading the material sequentially from the first chapter. Advanced readers may directly jump to any relevant chapter for reference; each chapter is self contained and provides further pointers to existing research.

We enjoyed writing this book and gained new insights in the process that we've shared in this material. We sincerely wish we had more time, in which case we would have been able to add more depth on several directly related topics. For example, the user-interface aspects of data cleaning have not received due attention in this book.

Venkatesh Ganti and Anish Das Sarma
September 2013

Preface

Acknowledgments

The structure and material in this book has been significantly influenced by people that both of us have worked with closely on several topics related to data cleaning. Prominently, some of them are Surajit Chaudhuri, Raghav Kaushik, Arvind Arasu, Eugene Agichtein, and Sunita Sarawagi. We are grateful to Tamer Ozsu and the publisher for the opportunity to explain our view on data cleaning in this book.

We also thank our families for their patience while we spent long hours outside of work writing this book, which should have been devoted to them instead.

Venkatesh Ganti and Anish Das Sarma
April 2013

CHAPTER 1

Introduction

Databases are ubiquitous in enterprise systems, and form the backbone for systems keeping track of business transactions and operational data. They also have become the defacto standard for supporting data analysis tasks generating reports indicating the health of the business operations. These reports are often critical to track performance as well as to make informed decisions on several issues confronting a business. The reporting functionality has become so important on its own that businesses often create consolidated data repositories. These repositories can be observed in several scenarios such as data warehousing for analysis, as well as for supporting sophisticated applications such as comparison shopping.

1.1 ENTERPRISE DATA WAREHOUSE

Data warehouses are large data repositories recording interactions between various entities that an enterprise deals with: customers, products, geographies, etc. By consolidating most of the relevant data describing the interactions into one repository, data warehouses facilitate canned and adhoc data analysis over such interactions.

The results of such analysis queries often form the backbone of several critical reports, which help evaluate and monitor performance of various business projects. These reports may often be useful for prioritizing among various business initiatives. Therefore, accuracy of data in these data warehouses is critical. Errors in these databases can result in significant downstream reporting errors. Sometimes, such errors can result in bad decisions being taken by the executives.

Errors in data tend to creep in from a variety of sources, say when new sales records are inserted. For instance, enterprises routinely obtain resellers' sales interactions with customers from resellers. Data entry at the point of sales is often performed in a rush and causes many errors in data. Sometimes, these errors are introduced because the sales agent does not try to find out the correct data, and enters a default or a typical value. So, the data about the customer sent by the reseller may not match with the current record in the data warehouse.

Alternatively, a large number of errors are often introduced into the data warehouse when data from a new source database is merged with it. Such data consolidation is required when sales transactions from a new data feed (say, an OLTP database) are inserted into the data warehouse. If some of the new records in both the source and target describe the same entities, then it is often possible that the data merger results in several data quality issues because interactions with the same entity are now distributed across multiple records.

1.2 COMPARISON SHOPPING DATABASE

Many popular comparison shopping search engines (e.g., Bing Shopping, Google Products, ShopZilla) are backed by comprehensive product catalog and offer databases consisting, respectively, of products and offers from multiple merchants to sell them at specific prices. The catalog and offer databases enable a comparison shopping engine to display products relevant to a user's search query and for each product the offers from various merchants. These databases are populated and maintained by assimilating feeds from both catalog providers (such as CNet, PriceGrabber) as well as from merchants (e.g., NewEgg.com, TigerDirect.com). These feeds are consolidated into a master catalog along with any other information per product received from merchants or from other sources. When a user searches for a product or a category of products, these comparison shopping sites display a set of top-ranking items for the specific user query. When a user is interested in a specific product, the user is then shown the list of merchants along with offers for each of them.

These product catalog and merchant feeds are obtained from independently developed databases. Therefore, identifiers and descriptions of the same product and those in the corresponding offers will very likely be different across each of the input feeds. Reconciling these differences is crucial for enabling a compelling useful comparison shopping experience to a user. Otherwise, information about the same product would be split across multiple records in the master catalog. Whichever record is shown to the user, the user is only shown a part of the information in the master catalog about the product. Therefore, one of the main goals is to maintain a correctly consolidated master catalog where each product sold at several merchants has only one representation.

Similar data quality issues arise in the context of *Master Data Management (MDM)*. The goal of an MDM system is to maintain a unified view of non-transactional data entities (e.g., customers, products) of an enterprise. Like in the data warehousing and comparison shopping scenarios, these master databases often grow through incremental or batch insertion of new entities. Thus, the same issues and challenges of maintaining a high data quality also arise in the context of master data management.

1.3 DATA CLEANING TASKS

Data cleaning is an overloaded term, and is often used loosely to refer to a variety of tasks aimed at improving the quality of data. Often, these tasks may have to be accomplished by stitching together multiple operations. We now discuss some common data cleaning tasks to better understand the underlying operations. We note that this list includes commonly encountered tasks, and is not comprehensive.

1.4 RECORD MATCHING

Informally, the goal of record matching is to match each record from a set of records with records in another table. Often, this task needs to be accomplished when a new set of entities is imported to the target relation to make sure that the insertion does not introduce duplicate entities in the target relation.

Enterprise Data Warehousing Scenario: Consider a scenario when a new batch of customer records is being imported into a sales database. In this scenario, it is important to verify whether or not the same customer is represented in both the existing as well as the incoming sets and only retain one record in the final result. Due to representational differences and errors, records in both batches could be different and may not match exactly on their key attributes (e.g., name and address or the CustomerId). The goal of a record matching task is to identify record pairs, one in each of two input relations, which correspond to the same real-world entity. Challenges to be addressed in this task include (i) identification of criteria under which two records represent the same real-world entity, and (ii) efficient computation strategies to determine such pairs over large input relations.

Table 1.1: Two sets of customer records

ID	Name	Street	City	Phone
r1	Sweetlegal Investments Inc	202 North	Redmond	425-444-5555
r2	ABC Groceries Corp	Amphitheatre Pkwy	Mountain View	4081112222
r3	Cable television services	One Oxford Dr	Cambridge	617-123-4567
s1	Sweet legal Invesments Incorporated	202 N	Redmond	
s2	ABC Groceries Corpn.	Amphitheetre Parkway	Mountain View	
s3	Cable Services	One Oxford Dr	Cambridge	6171234567

Comparison Shopping Scenario: Recall the comparison shopping scenario, where the target comparison shopping site maintains a master catalog of products. Suppose a merchant sends a new feed of products, as shown in Table 1.2. Each of these products has to be matched with a target in the master, or if there is no such matching product, add it as a new product to the master catalog.

Ideally, the merchant could also send a unique identifier that matches a global identifier in the master catalog. In the case of books, ISBN is an identifier that everyone agrees to and uses. However, in other categories of products, there is no such global identifier that can be used for matching. The main challenge here is that the description often used by the merchant may not match with the description at the target comparison shopping site. Hence, matching products "correctly" requires several challenges to be addressed.

The hardness is further exacerbated in the case of products where the underlying product description is often a concatenation of several attribute values. The individual values may themselves be equal while the concatenation of these values in different orders could cause the two strings to look very different.

Table 1.2: Product catalog with a new set of products

ID	Title
r1	Canon EOS 20D Digital SLR Body Kit (Req. Lens) USA
r2	Nikon D90 SLR
s1	Canon EOS 20d Digital Camera Body USA - Lens sold separately
s2	Nikon D90 SLR Camera

Record matching is discussed further in Chapter 7.

1.5 SCHEMA MATCHING

A task that often precedes record matching is that of *Schema Matching*: the task of aligning attributes from different schemas. As an example, suppose the information from our warehouse example were organized as a relation $R(Name, CityAddress, Country, Phone, \ldots)$, which stores most of the address (except Country) in a single attribute in textual format. Now suppose you obtain another relation with data represented in the format $S(Company, Apt, Street, City, Zip, Nation, PhoneNumber)$, which breaks the address into individual components. To populate tuples in S into R, we need a process to *convert* each S tuple into the format of R. Schema matching provides: (1) *attribute correspondences* describing which attributes in S correspond to attributes in R; e.g., Country corresponds to Nation, PhoneNumber corresponds to Phone, Company corresponds to Name, and City Address corresponds to the remaining four attributes in S (2) *transformation functions* give concrete functions to obtain attribute values in R from attribute values in S; e.g., a transformation process gives a mechanism to concatenate all attributes to form City Address (or extract attributes like Zip code when converting R to S).

Schema matching is discussed along with record matching in Chapter 7.

1.6 DEDUPLICATION

The goal of *deduplication* is to group records in a table such that each group of records represents the same entity. The deduplication operation is often required when a database is being populated or cleaned the first time.

Informally, the difference between deduplication and record matching is that deduplication involves an additional grouping of "matching" records, such that the groups collectively partition the input relation. Since record matching is typically not transitive (i.e., record pairs $(r1, r2)$

and $(r2, r3)$ may be considered matches but $(r1, r3)$ may not be), the grouping poses additional technical challenges.

For example, consider the enterprise data warehousing scenario. When the data warehouse is first populated from various feeds, it is possible that the same customer could be represented by multiple records in one feed, and even more records across feeds. So, it is important for all records representing the same customer to be reconciled. In Table 1.3, records {g11, g12, g13} are "duplicate" records of each other while {g21, g31} is another set of duplicate records.

Table 1.3: Table showing records with {g11, g12, g13} being one group of duplications, and {g21, g31} another set of duplicate records

ID	Name	Street	City	Phone
g11	Sweetlegal Investments Inc	202 North	Redmond	425-444-5555
g12	Sweet legal Invesments Incorporated	202 N	Redmond	
g13	Sweetlegal Inc	202 N	Redmond	
g21	ABC Groceries Corp	Amphitheatre Pkwy	Mountain View	4081112222
g31	Cable television services	One Oxford Dr	Cambridge	617-123-4567

Let us consider the task of maintaining a shopping catalog in the comparison shopping scenario. Once again, it is possible that a set of records received from a merchant may have multiple records representing the same entity. In the following Table 1.4, {g21, g22, g23, g24} all represent the same entity, a Nikon DSLR camera.

Table 1.4: Table showing grouping, with {g21, g22, g23, g24} all representing the same entity, a Nikon DSLR camera

ID	Title
g1	Canon EOS 20D Digital SLR Body Kit (Req. Lens) USA
g21	Nikon D90 SLR
g22	Nikon D90 SLR Camera
g23	Nikon D90
g24	D90 SLR

Deduplication is discussed in detail in Chapter 8.

1.7 DATA STANDARDIZATION

Consider a scenario where a relation contains several customer records with missing zip code or state values, or improperly formatted street address strings. It is important to fill in missing values and adjust the format of the address strings so as to return correct results for analysis queries. For instance, if a business analyst wants to understand the number of customers for a specific product by zip code, it is important for all customer records to have the correct zip code values.

The same task is also often required in the maintenance of product catalog databases. For example, ensuring that all dimensions for a set of products are expressed in the same units, and that these attribute values are not missing is very important. Otherwise, search queries on these attributes may not return correct results.

The task of ensuring that all attribute values are "standardized" as per the same conventions is often called *data standardization*.

Data standardization is often a critical operation required before other data cleaning tasks such as record matching or deduplication. Standardizing the format and correcting attribute values leads to significantly better accuracy in other data cleaning tasks such as record matching and deduplication.

1.8 DATA PROFILING

The process of cleansing data is often an iterative and continuous process. It is important to *evaluate* quality of data in a database before one initiates data cleansing process, and subsequently assesses its success. The process of evaluating data quality is called *data profiling*, and typically involves gathering several aggregate data statistics which constitute the data profile. An informal goal of data quality is to ensure that the values match up with expectations. For example, one may expect the customer name and address columns uniquely determine each customer record in a Customer relation. In such a case, the number of unique [name, address] values must be close to that of the total number of records in the Customer relation.

A subset of elements of a data profile may each be obtained using one or more SQL queries. However, the data profile of a database may also consist of a large number of such elements. Hence, computing them all together efficiently is an important challenge here. Also, some of the data profile elements (say, identifying histograms of attribute values which satisfy certain regular expressions) may not easily be computed using SQL queries.

1.9 FOCUS OF THIS BOOK

In this book, we focus our discussion on solutions for data cleaning tasks. However, data cleaning is just one of the goals in an enterprise data management system. For instance, a typical *extract-transform-load (ETL)* process also encompasses several other tasks some of which transform data from sources into the desired schema at the target before merging all data into the target. In this survey, we do not discuss all the goals of ETL.

In particular, we do not discuss the topic of data transformation which is one of the goals of ETL. We also do not discuss the issue of data or information integration, which also requires transforming (perhaps, dynamically) the source data into the schema required by the user's query, besides data cleaning.

CHAPTER 2

Technological Approaches

In this chapter, we discuss common technological approaches for developing data cleaning solutions. Several approaches exist to enable the development and deployment of effective solutions for data cleaning. These approaches differ primarily in the flexibility and the effort required from the developer implementing the data cleaning solution. The more flexible approaches often require the developer to implement significant parts of the solution, while the less flexible are often easier to deploy provided they meet the solution's requirements.

2.1 DOMAIN-SPECIFIC VERTICALS

The first category consists of verticals such as Trillium `http://www.trilliumsoftware.com/` that provide data cleaning functionality for specific domains. Since they understand the domain where the vertical is being applied they can tune their solution for the given domain. However, by design, these are not generic and hence cannot be applied to other domains.

The main advantage of these domain-specific solutions is that they can incorporate knowledge of the domain while developing the solution. Because the domain is known, the flow of operations to be performed are often decidable upfront. Hence, these solutions can often be comprehensive and are easier to deploy. For example, a data cleaning package for addresses can incorporate the format of a typical address record. In fact, they often try to "standardize" the formats of address records in that they transform input records to a standard format specific to a location. Subsequent operations are then applied to these standardized records. Such data transformations require knowledge about the input data characteristics, and often are only available for domain-specific solutions.

The downside of this approach of developing domain-specific solutions is that they are not generic and cannot be ported to other domains. For example, a solution developed for U.S. addresses cannot be applied to the domain of electronic products, because the characteristics of the data are very different across these two domains. Sometimes, the solutions are also sensitive to sub-categories within a domain. For instance, a solution for U.S. addresses may not be applied to clean the addresses from India or other Asian countries because the data characteristics across these countries are significantly different.

2.2 GENERIC PLATFORMS

The second category of approaches relies on horizontal ETL Platforms such as Microsoft SQL Server Integration Services (SSIS – http://msdn.microsoft.com/sql) and IBM Websphere Information Integration. These platforms provide a suite of operators including relational operators such as select, project, and equi-join. A common feature across these frameworks is extensibility, where applications can plug in their own custom operators. These platforms provide support to implement the data and control flow easily, and to execute the resulting program efficiently. A data transformation and cleaning solution is built by composing the default and custom operators to obtain an operator tree or a graph. This extensible operator-centric approach is also adopted in research initiatives such as Ajax and Morpheus.

While this category of software can in principle support arbitrarily complex logic by virtue of being extensible, it has the obvious limitation that most of the data cleaning logic potentially needs to be incorporated as custom components. And, creating such optimized custom components for data cleaning software is nontrivial. Therefore, this approach requires significant amount of effort from developers.

2.3 OPERATOR-BASED APPROACH

The third approach builds upon the extensible ETL platforms by extending their repertoire of the default operators beyond traditional relational operators with a few core data cleaning operators such that with much less extra effort and code, we can obtain a rich variety of efficient and effective data cleaning solutions. The advantages of this approach include those of retaining much of the flexibility of the generic ETL platforms while also having the heavy lifting done by the optimized but flexible data cleaning operators. So, effective solutions can be relatively easily developed. Note that, however, solutions still have to be developed for any given domain and scenario.

This approach is similar to query processing, which derives its power from compositionality over a few basic operators, and is in sharp contrast with the earlier approaches which focused on the development of monolithic data cleaning solutions. The challenge however would be to identify such generic data cleaning operators which can then be customized to build solutions for specific domains and scenarios.

2.4 GENERIC DATA CLEANING OPERATORS

We continue the discussion on the operator-centric approach for developing data cleaning solutions. The goal is to identify and define a few critical operators, which can be used (along with standard relational operators) to build fairly general and accurate data cleaning solutions. As an analogy, consider relational database systems where a very rich set of queries can be posed using very few primitive operators. We can take a similar approach for data cleaning as well and enable easy programmability of data cleaning solutions over a basic set of primitive data cleaning operators and relational operators. The primitive operators may be implemented within extensible horizontal platforms such as IBM Ascential, SQL Server Integration Services or even database query processing engines to achieve the power through compositionality with other relational operators.

We now informally introduce a few critical primitive operators. We discuss each of these in detail in subsequent chapters.

2.4.1 SIMILARITY JOIN

A very important data cleaning operation is that of "joining" similar data. This operation is useful in record matching as well as deduplication. For example, consider a sales data warehouse. Owing to various errors in the data due to typing mistakes, differences in conventions, etc., product names and customer names in sales records may not match exactly with master product catalog and reference customer registration records respectively. In these situations, it would be desirable to perform similarity joins. For instance, we may join two products (respectively, customers) if the similarity between their part descriptions (respectively, customer names and addresses) is high. This problem of joining similar data has been studied in the context of record linkage, of identifying approximate duplicate entities in databases. It is also relevant when identifying for a given record the best few approximate matches from among a reference set of records. The similarity join is the fundamental operation upon which many of these techniques are built.

Current approaches exploit similarity between attribute values to join data across relations, e.g., similarities in part descriptions in the above example. A variety of string similarity functions have been considered, such as edit distance, jaccard similarity, cosine similarity, and generalized edit distance, for measuring similarities. However, no single string similarity function is known to be the overall best similarity function, and the choice usually depends on the application domain. For example, the characteristics of an effective similarity function for matching products based on their part names where the errors are usually spelling errors would be different from those matching street addresses because even small differences in the street numbers such as "148th Ave" and "147th Ave" are crucial, and the soundex function for matching person names. Therefore, we need a similarity join operator that employs customizable similarity functions.

2.4.2 CLUSTERING

Clustering is another critical operation that is useful in many data cleaning tasks. Informally speaking, clustering refers to the operation of taking a set of items, and putting them into smaller groups based on "similarity." For example, a list of restaurants may be clustered based on similar cuisines, or based on their price, or some combination of price and cuisine. Clustering is often used in a pre-processing step of deduplication called *blocking*: When the set of records to be deduplicated is very large, blocking performs a crude clustering to bring similar "blocks" of records together, and a finer-grained pairwise comparison is only performed within each block. Another application of clustering is in deduplication itself. Once we have pairwise similarities between pairs of records in a block, clustering based on the pairwise similarities is used to obtain the final deduplicated set of records.

In addition to the "similarity" measure, clustering may be guided by *constraints* that restrict which set of items may or may not be grouped together, and an *objective function* that determines the best possible clustering among all that satisfy the constraints. Chapter 5 gives a formal definition of clustering, and how constraints and objective functions are modeled. We then present two main approaches to clustering: (1) A hash-based approach where each item is placed in a cluster based on the value it produces based on some hash function; (2) a graph-based approach that translates the clustering problem into finding structures in a graph.

2.4.3 PARSING

The differences in schema between the source and destination databases often makes the data cleaning operations such as record matching and deduplication fairly challenging. Due to these schema differences, an attribute at the source may actually correspond to a concatenation of attribute values at the destination schema. In such cases, it becomes important to "parse" the attribute values from the source into the corresponding attribute values at the destination.

Consider a scenario where a customer relation is being imported to add new records to a target customer relation. Suppose the address information in the target relation is split into its constituent attributes [street address, city, state, and zip code] while in the source relation they are all concatenated into one attribute. Before the records from the source relation could be inserted in the target relation, it is essential to segment each address value in the source relation to identify the attribute values at the target.

For example, an input address string "15633 148th Ave Bellevue WA 98004" has to be split into the following sub-components before populating the destination table.

```
House Number : 15633 Street Name : 148th Ave.
City : Bellevue
State : WA Zip : 98004
```

The goal of a *parsing* task is to split an incoming string into segments each of which may be inserted as attribute values at the target. Informally:

Definition 2.1 Parsing. Given a string text T and a relation schema $\mathcal{S} = \{A_1, \ldots, A_n\}$, the goal of parsing is to construct a tuple t with schema $\mathcal{S}$ from T subject to the constraint that t is considered a valid and accurate tuple in the target relation.

A significant challenge to be addressed by this task is to efficiently and accurately identify sub-strings of an input string which form the attribute values of the destination schema.

Such scenarios also arise in the context of product databases where the source may not have split individual attribute values, say, the main technical attributes of a digital camera (zoom, focal length, etc.). Note that some product attribute parsing scenarios may require the following generalization. The generalization involves the extraction of individual attribute values from an input string but with the following relaxation: not all of the input string is consumed by individual attribute values.

2.5 BIBLIOGRAPHY

An example of a fairly comprehensive data cleaning solution for a specific vertical is that of Trillium address cleansing software. Examples for ETL platforms that enable users to utilize existing operators along with the incorporation of custom operators include IBM Data Integration (http://www-01.ibm.com/software/data/integration/) and Microsoft SQL Server Integration Services. The proposals for operator-centric approaches for data cleaning and ETL have been made in several research projects, e.g., [Chaudhuri et al., 2006a, Dohzen et al., 2006, Galhardas et al., 2000].

CHAPTER 3

Similarity Functions

A common requirement in several critical data cleaning operations is to measure the closeness between pairs of records. *Similarity functions* (or, *similarity measures*) between atomic values constituting a record form the backbone of measuring closeness between records.

No single similarity function is universally applicable across all domains and scenarios. For example the characteristics of an effective similarity function for comparing products based on their part names—where the errors are typically spelling errors—would only pardon a few characters being misspelt. However, in the context of names being entered into a web form based on phone conversations, or voice detection systems, even large differences in the spellings with similar pronunciations (e.g., "Rupert" and "Robert") may be considered very similar. So, several similarity functions are required and have been used.

In the subsequent sections, we enumerate various similarity functions that have been explored in the context of data cleaning tasks, and illustrate them using examples. Our goal is to present a list of popularly used similarity functions, with a focus on string similarity, and our list is by no means comprehensive. In Section 3.6, we present a brief bibliography on the topic.

3.1 EDIT DISTANCE

One of the most commonly used string similarity measures is based on *edit distance*, also known as the Levenshtein distance: Given two strings $s1$ and $s2$, the *edit distance* (denoted $ed(s1, s2)$) between the strings is given by the number of "edit" operations required to transform $s1$ to $s2$ (or vice versa). The edit distance is defined by a set of edit operations that are allowed for the transformation. Typical edit operations are *insert*, *delete*, and *replacement* of one character at any position in the string.

Definition 3.1 Given two strings σ_1 and σ_2, the *edit distance* $ED(\sigma_1, \sigma_2)$ between them is the minimum number of edit operations—insertion, deletion, and replacement—to transform σ_1 into σ_2. We define the *edit similarity* $ES(\sigma_1, \sigma_2)$ to be $1.0 - \frac{ED(\sigma_1,\sigma_2)}{max(|\sigma_1|,|\sigma_2|)}$.

Example 3.2 Consider strings $s1$ ="Sweet" and $s2$ ="Sweat." If we only consider the insert and delete edit operations, we can translate $s1$ to $s2$ by first deleting the fourth character 'e', and then inserting 'a' at the same position. Since we needed two edit operations, the edit distance between $s1$ and $s2$ is two. With the replacement operation allowed, the edit distance between $s1$ and $s2$ in the example above becomes one.

A further generalization of the edit distance incorporates *costs* (or *weights*) on edit operations. Each edit operation incurs a positive cost, and the cost of a sequence of operations is given by the sum of costs of each operation in the sequence. Then, the edit distance between two strings is given by the cost of the cost-minimizing sequence of edit operations that translates one string to another.

Example 3.3 Let us again consider strings $s1 =$"Sweet" and $s2 =$"Sweat." Suppose we have three edit operations: insert and delete with a cost of 2 and replacement with a cost of 3. Now the edit distance between $s1$ and $s2$ is three, since we can transform $s1$ to $s2$ with one edit. Note that using a delete followed by an insert will incur a cost of 4.

Note that depending on the set and costs of operations allowed, the edit distance function may or may not be symmetric. However, we often use a slight modification that makes the function symmetric: the revised goal is to perform a sequence of transformations of least total cost on one or both of the strings $s1$ and $s2$ so as to reach some same string s.

3.2 JACCARD SIMILARITY

Another common string similarity measure is based on the well-known *jaccard set similarity*. Informally, the jaccard similarity is the ratio of the size of the intersection over the size of the union. Hence, two sets that have a lot of elements in common are closer to each other.

Definition 3.4 Let $S1$ and $S2$ be two sets.

1. The jaccard containment of $S1$ in $S2$, $JC(S1, S2)$ is defined to be $\frac{|S1 \cap S2|}{|S1|}$.
2. The jaccard similarity between $S1$ and $S2$, $JR(S1, S2)$, is defined to be $\frac{|S1 \cap S2|}{|S1 \cup S2|}$.

The above definition can be extended to also consider weighted sets by replacing the sizes of the various sets (including those obtained by intersection and union) with their weighted counterparts.

To apply the jaccard set similarity between two strings, we need to transform the two input strings $s1$ and $s2$ into sets. A standard approach for this conversion is to obtain the set of all q-*grams* of the input string: A q-gram is a contiguous sequence of q characters in the input. Given the two input strings $s1$ and $s2$, we obtain all q-grams of each string to obtain sets $Q(s1)$ and $Q(s2)$. The similarity between $s1$ and $s2$ is then given by the jaccard similarity $J(Q(s1), Q(s2))$ between the two sets of q-grams.

Example 3.5 Let us again consider strings $s1 =$"Sweet" and $s2 =$"Sweat." Using $q = 2$, we obtain $Q(s1) = \{Sw, we, ee, et\}$ and $Q(s2) = \{Sw, we, ea, at\}$. Therefore, we have the similarity between $s1$ and $s2$ given by $J(Q(s1), Q(s2)) = \frac{|Q(s1) \cap Q(s2)|}{|Q(s1) \cup Q(s2)|} = \frac{1}{3}$.

Q-grams based jaccard similarities are very useful in slightly longer strings, such as addresses or documents.

There are many variants of jaccard-based similarity, such as incorporating edit distances or synonyms into the jaccard distance. For instance, we may consider forming sets of tokens from the input strings, and then modifying the jaccard similarity by also considering synonyms as being equal in the set union/intersection computation. Another common approach is to assign weights to q-grams based on IDF. We could compute the IDF of each relevant q-gram directly based on the set of all q-grams for a given set of strings; another alternative is to inherit the IDF of the parent token from which the q-gram is derived and applying an aggregate function in cases where a q-gram appears in multiple tokens.

3.3 COSINE SIMILARITY

Cosine similarity is a vector-based similarity measure between strings where the input strings $s1$ and $s2$ are translated to vectors in a high-dimensional space. Informally, closer strings are also closer to each other in the vector space. Typically, the transformation of the input strings to vectors is done based on the tokens that appear in the string, with each token corresponding to a dimension and the frequency of the token in the input being the weight of the vector in that dimension. The string similarity is then given by the cosine similarity of the two vectors (i.e., the cosine of the angle between the two vectors).

Example 3.6 Consider strings $s1 =$"Sweet Inc" and $s2 =$"Sweet." Assuming each token is a different dimension and treating "Sweet" as the first dimension and "Inc" as the second, we get the following vectors: $v(s1) = \{1, 1\}$ and $v(s2) = \{1, 0\}$. Computing the cosine of the angle (45 degrees) between these two vectors, we get a similarity between $s1$ and $s2$ to be 0.707.

Cosine similarity is typically useful for larger strings such as web documents, addresses, or text records. To avoid high-dimensionality and noise due to irrelevant words, *stop-words* (such as "the," "an," etc.), and commonly occurring words are often eliminated before constructing the two vectors.

3.4 SOUNDEX

Soundex is a phonetic approach for measuring the similarity between strings. The idea is to convert any string to some code based on the pronunciation of the word, and then compare the codes of the strings. The exact method for conversion of strings to the code depends on the variant of the language being used, but a common approach for American English is as follows (see http://en.wikipedia.org/wiki/Soundex):

- Retain the first letter of the string and drop all other occurrences of all a, e, i, o, u, y, h, w.
- Replace consonants with numbers as per the following mapping:

    - b, f, p, v ⇒ 1
    - c, g, j, k, q, s, x, z ⇒ 2
    - d, t ⇒ 3
    - l ⇒ 4
    - m, n ⇒ 5
    - r ⇒ 6

- The following constraints are applied in the replacement described in the step above:
    - If more than one consecutive letters (before elimination of letters described in the first step above) get replaced to the same number, only retain the first number. Further, if such letters were separated by 'h' or 'w', still retain only one number.
    - However, if two such letters are separated by a vowel, retain both numbers in the code.
- Retain the first letter and the subsequent three numbers to obtain the code for the string. If there are fewer than three numbers, append 0s at the end.

Example 3.7 Using the approach described above, "Robert" and "Rupert" get converted to the same code "R163."

3.5 COMBINATIONS AND LEARNING SIMILARITY FUNCTIONS

Each of the similarity measures is most suitable for certain types of strings, and no single string similarity measure is perfect for any pair of strings. Therefore, we commonly need to combine multiple string similarities, such as using a linear weighted combination. Given some training data, one can use standard machine-learning algorithms to learn a suitable combined similarity function for a given dataset.

3.6 BIBLIOGRAPHY

String similarity has a long history with lots of past work. Therefore, we don't provide a comprehensive reference here. Instead, we refer the reader to the surveys by Koudas et al. [2006], and by Cohen et al. [2003]. These surveys study and compare several similarity functions, even beyond the ones discussed in this chapter. Further, the SecondString similarity package (http://secondstring.sourceforge.net/) is a very useful practical string similarity library.

CHAPTER 4

Operator: Similarity Join

Recall that the goal of the record matching task is to match pairs of records across two relations. The matching function may involve several predicates. However, one of the crucial predicates often is to measure closeness in terms of textual context between records. This similarity is often quantified by a textual similarity function which compares the content of the two records. There are a variety of common similarity functions as discussed in the previous chapter. As in record matching, the deduplication task typically involves many predicates. However, a critical one is often based on textual similarity between records.

In this chapter, we discuss the *similarity join* operator, which forms the backbone of both the record matching and deduplication tasks. The goal of the similarity join is to identify all pairs of very similar records across two relations, where the similarity between records is measured by a customizable similarity function. The similarity join can be expressed as a relational join where the join condition is specified using the given similarity function as follows.

Definition 4.1 The *similarity join* of two relations R and S, both containing a column A, is the join $R \bowtie_\theta S$ where the join predicate θ is $sim(R.A, S.A) > \alpha$, for a given similarity function sim and a threshold α.

Although similarity joins may be expressed in SQL by defining join predicates through user-defined functions (UDFs), their evaluation would be very inefficient as database systems usually are forced to apply UDF-based join predicates only after performing a cross product. We introduce the *Set-Similarity Join (SSJoin)* operator, which is a basic primitive and show that it can be used for supporting similarity joins based on several string similarity functions (e.g., edit similarity, jaccard similarity, hamming distance, soundex, as well as similarity based on co-occurrences), some of which we saw in the previous chapter.

4.1 SET SIMILARITY JOIN (SSJOIN)

In defining the SSJoin operator, we exploit the following observations:

1. As we saw in the previous chapter, there are several well-known methods of mapping a string to a set, such as the set of words partitioned by delimiters, the set of all substrings of length q, i.e., its constituent *q-grams*, etc. For example, the string "Sweetlegal Investments" could be treated as a set of words $'Sweetlegal','Investments'\}$ or as a set of 3-grams,

{'Swe', 'wee', 'eet', 'etl', 'tle', 'leg', 'ega', 'gal', 'al ', '1 I', ' In', 'Inv', 'nve', 'ves', 'est', 'stm', 'tme', 'men', 'ent', 'nts'}.

2. The overlap between sets can be used to effectively support a variety of similarity functions; for example, we saw that cosine similarity and jaccard similarity defined in the previous chapter fall in this category.

The SSJoin operator compares values based on sets associated with (or explicitly constructed for) each input string. Henceforth, we refer to the set corresponding to a string σ as $Set(\sigma)$. This set could be obtained by any method, including the aforementioned ones. Also, whenever we refer to sets, we mean multi-sets. Hence, when we refer to the union and intersection of sets, we mean the multi-set union and multi-set intersection respectively.

In general, elements may be associated with weights. This is intended to capture the intuition that different portions of a string have different importance. For example, in the string "Sweetlegal Investments," we may want to associate more importance to the portion "Sweetlegal." There are well-known methods of associating weights to the set elements, such as the notion of Inverse Document Frequency (IDF) commonly used in Information Retrieval. We assume that the weight associated with an element of a set, such as a word or q-gram, is fixed and that it is positive. Formally, all sets are assumed to be drawn from a universe $\mathcal{U}$. Each distinct value in $\mathcal{U}$ is associated with a unique *weight*. The weight of a set s is defined to be the sum of the weights of its members and is denoted as $wt(s)$. Henceforth, in this chapter, we talk about weighted sets, noting that in the special case when all weights are equal to 1, we reduce to the unweighted case.

Given two sets s_1, s_2, we define their *overlap similarity*, denoted $Overlap(s_1, s_2)$, to be the weight of their intersection, i.e., $wt(s_1 \cap s_2)$. The overlap similarity between two strings, σ_1, σ_2, $Overlap(\sigma_1, \sigma_2)$ is defined as $Overlap(Set(\sigma_1), Set(\sigma_2))$.

Example 4.2 Consider strings "Sweetlegal Investments" and "Sweeltegal Investment." Consider the corresponding sets of 3-grams, {'Swe', 'wee', 'eet', 'etl', 'tle', 'leg', 'ega', 'gal', 'al ', '1 I', ' In', 'Inv', 'nve', 'ves', 'est', 'stm', 'tme', 'men', 'ent', 'nts'} and {'Swe', 'wee', 'eet', 'elt', 'lte', 'leg', 'ega', 'gal', 'al ', '1 I', ' In', 'Inv', 'nve', 'ves', 'est', 'stm', 'tme', 'men', 'ent'}. Assume all weights are 1. The overlap similarity between the two strings is the size of the intersection of the two sets of 3-grams, which is 17.

Given relations R and S, each with string valued attribute A, consider the similarity join between R and S that returns all pairs of tuples where the overlap similarity between $R.A$ and $S.A$ is above a certain threshold. We expect that when two strings are almost equal, their overlap similarity is high, and hence this is a natural similarity join predicate to express. We next introduce the SSJoin operator that can be used to express this predicate.

We shall use the standard relational data model for simplicity of presentation. However, the techniques described in this chapter are also applicable to other models allowing inline representation of set-valued attributes. We assume that all relations are in the First Normal Form, and do

Orgname	3-gram	Norm	Orgname	3-gram	Norm
Sweetlegal Investments	Swe	20	Sweeltegal Investment	Swe	19
Sweetlegal Investments	wee	20	Sweeltegal Investment	wee	19
...	...	...	...	...	...
Sweetlegal Investments	nts	20	Sweeltegal Investment	ent	19

Figure 4.1: Example sets from strings.

not contain set-valued attributes. Sets and hence the association between a string and its set are also represented in a normalized manner. For example, the set of rows in relation R of Figure 4.1 represents the association between the string "Sweetlegal Investments" and its 3-grams; the third *Norm* column denotes the length of the string.

We describe the SSJoin operator next. Consider relations $R(A, B)$ and $S(A, B)$ where A and B are subsets of columns. Each distinct value $a_r \in R.A$ defines a group, which is the subset of tuples in R where $R.A = a_r$. Call this set of tuples $Set(a_r)$. Similarly, each distinct value $a_s \in S.A$ defines a set $Set(a_s)$. The simplest form of the SSJoin operator joins a pair of distinct values $\langle a_r, a_s \rangle$, $a_r \in R.A$ and $a_s \in S.A$, if the projections on column B of the sets $Set(a_r)$ and $Set(a_s)$ have a high overlap similarity. The formal predicate is $Overlap(\ _B(Set(a_r)),\ _B(Set(a_s))) \quad \phi$ for some threshold ϕ. We denote $Overlap(\ _B(Set(a_r)),\ _B(Set(a_s)))$ as $Overlap_B(a_r, a_s)$. Hence, the formal predicate is $Overlap_B(a_r, a_s) \quad \phi$. We illustrate this through an example.

Example 4.3 Let relation $R(OrgName, 3\text{-}gram, Norm)$ and $S(OrgName, 3\text{-}gram, Norm)$ shown in Figure 4.1 associate the strings "Sweetlegal Investments" and "Sweeltegal Investment" with their 3-grams. Denoting *OrgName* by A and *3-gram* by B, the SSJoin operator with the predicate $Overlap_B(a_r, a_s) \quad 15$ returns the pair of strings ⟨"Sweetlegal Investments," "Sweeltegal Investment"⟩ since the overlap between the corresponding sets of 3-grams is 10.

In general, we may wish to express conditions such as: the overlap similarity between the two sets must be 80% of the set size, akin to the jaccard string similarity measure we have seen. Thus, in the above example, we may wish to assert that the overlap similarity must be higher than 80% of the number of 3-grams in the string "Sweetlegal Investments." We may also wish to be able to assert that the overlap similarity be higher than say 80% of the sizes of *both* sets. We now formally define the SSJoin operator as follows, which addresses these requirements.

Definition 4.4 Consider relations $R(A, B)$ and $S(A, B)$. Let $pred$ be the predicate $\bigwedge_i \{Overlap_B(a_r, a_s) \quad e_i\}$, where each e_i is an expression involving only constants and columns from either $R.A$ or $S.A$. We write $R\ SSJoin_A^{pred}\ S$ to denote the following result: $\{\langle a_r, a_s\rangle \in R.A \times S.A | pred(a_r, a_s)$ is true $\}$.

We also write $pred$ as $\{Overlap_B(a_r, a_s) \geq e_i\}$.

We illustrate this through the following examples based on Figure 4.1. The third column *Norm* denotes the length of the string. In general, the *norm* denotes either the length of the string, or the cardinality of the set, or the sum of the weights of all elements in the set. Several similarity functions use the norm to normalize the similarity.

Example 4.5 As shown in Figure 4.1, let relations $R(OrgName, 3\text{-}gram, Norm)$ and $S(OrgName, 3, Norm)$ associate the organization names with (1) all 3-grams in each organization name, and (2) the number of 3-grams for each name. The predicate in the SSJoin operator may be instantiated in one of the following ways to derive different notions of similarity.

- Absolute overlap: $Overlap_B(a_r, a_s) \geq 15$ joins the pair of strings ⟨"Sweetlegal Investments," "Sweeltegal Investment"⟩ since the overlap between the corresponding sets of 3-grams is 17.
- 1-sided normalized overlap: $Overlap_B(\langle a, norm\rangle_r, \langle a, norm\rangle_s) \geq 0.80 \cdot R.norm$ joins the pair of strings ⟨"Sweetlegal Investments," "Sweeltegal Investment"⟩ since the overlap between the corresponding sets of 3-grams is 17, which is more than 80% of 20.
- 2-sided normalized overlap: $Overlap_B(\langle a, norm\rangle_r, \langle a, norm\rangle_s) \geq \{0.8 \cdot R.norm, 0.8 \cdot S.norm\}$ also returns the pair of strings ⟨"Sweetlegal Investments," "Sweeltegal Investment"⟩ since 17 is more than 80% of 20 and 80% of 19.

In the next section, we show how the intuitive notion of set overlap can be used to capture various string similarity functions.

4.2 INSTANTIATIONS

In this section, we fix unary relations Rbase(A) and Sbase(A) where A is a string-valued attribute. The goal is to find pairs ⟨Rbase.A, Sbase.A⟩ where the textual similarity is above a threshold α. Our approach (outlined in Figure 4.2) is to first convert the strings Rbase(A) and Sbase(A) to sets, construct normalized representations $R(A, B, norm(A))$ and $S(A, B, norm(A))$, and then suitably invoke the SSJoin operator on the normalized representations. The invocation is chosen so that all string pairs whose similarity is greater than α are guaranteed to be in the result of the SSJoin operator. Hence, the SSJoin operator provides a way to efficiently produce a small superset of the correct answer. We then compare the pairs of strings using the actual similarity function, declared as a UDF within a database system, to ensure that we only return pairs of strings whose similarity is above α.

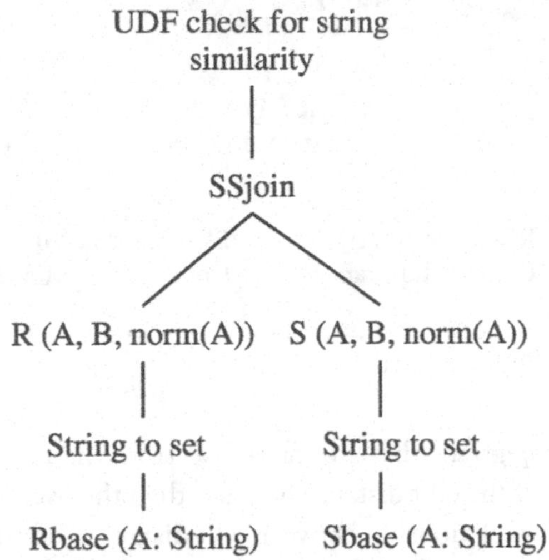

Figure 4.2: String similarity join using SSJoin.

Note that a direct implementation of the UDF within a database system is most likely to lead to a cross-product where the UDF is evaluated for all pairs of tuples. On the other hand, an implementation using SSJoin exploits the support within database systems for equi-joins to result in a significant reduction in the total number of string comparisons.

4.2.1 EDIT DISTANCE

As defined in Chapter 3, recall that the edit distance between strings is the least number of edit operations (insertion and deletion of characters, and replacement of a character with another) required to transform one string to the other. For example, the edit distance between strings 'sweetlegal' and 'sweeltegal' is 2, the number of edits (deleting and inserting 't') required to match the second string with the first. The edit distance may be normalized to be between 0 and 1 by the maximum of the two string lengths. Hence, the notion of edit similarity can also be defined as follows.

We consider the form of edit distance join that returns all pairs of records where the edit distance is less than an input threshold ϕ. This implementation can be easily extended to edit similarity joins. We illustrate the connection between edit distance and overlap through the following example.

Definition 4.6 Consider the strings "Sweetlegal Investments" and "Sweeltegal Investment." The edit distance between the two is 3 (deleting and inserting 't' and deleting 's'). The overlap similarity between their 3-grams is 17, more than 80% of the number of 3-grams in either string.

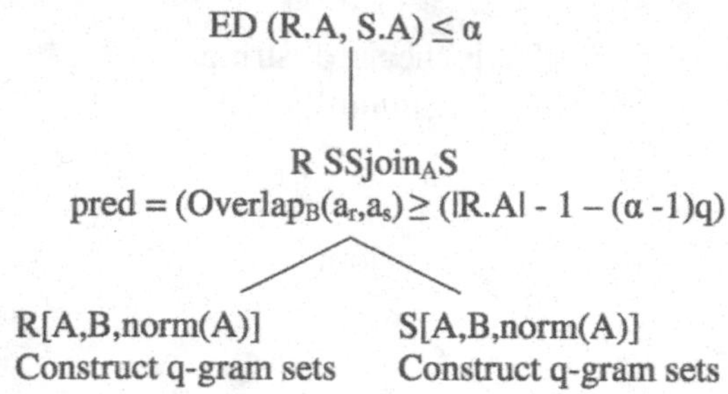

Figure 4.3: Edit distance join.

The intuition is all q-grams that are "far away" from the place where the edits take place must be identical. Hence, if the edit distance is small, then the overlap on q-grams must be high. We formalize this intuitive relationship between edit distance and the set of q-grams:

Property 4.7 Consider strings $_1$ and $_2$, of lengths $|\ _1|$ and $|\ _2|$, respectively. Let $QGSet_q(\ )$ denote the set of all contiguous q-grams of the string . If $_1$ and $_2$ are within an edit distance of τ, then $Overlap(QGSet_q(\ _1), QGSet_q(\ _2)) \quad \max(|\ _1|, |\ _2|) \quad q+1 \quad \tau\ q$

Thus, in the above example, the edit distance is 3, and Property 4.7 asserts that at least nine 3-grams have to be common.

From the above property, we can implement the edit similarity join through the operator tree shown in Figure 4.3. We first construct the relations $R(A, B, norm(A))$ and $S(A, B, norm(A))$ containing the norms and q-gram sets for each string. We then invoke the SSJoin operator over these relations in order to identify $\langle R.A, S.A\rangle$ pairs which are very similar. Note that we further require a filter based on edit similarity (possibly as a user-defined function) in order to filter out pairs whose overlap similarity is higher than that given by Property 4.7 but edit similarity is still less than the required threshold.

4.2.2 JACCARD CONTAINMENT AND SIMILARITY

As defined in Chapter 3, recall that the jaccard containment and similarity between strings is defined through the jaccard containment and similarity of their corresponding sets. We then illustrate the use of the SSJoin operator for jaccard containment using the following example.

Example 4.8 Suppose we define the jaccard containment between two strings by using the underlying sets of 3-grams. Consider strings $_1$ = "Sweetlegal Investments" and $_2$ = "Sweeltegal Investment." We show how a jaccard containment predicate on these strings translates to a SSJoin predicate. Suppose we want to join the two strings when the jaccard containment of $_1$ in $_2$ is more than 0.8.

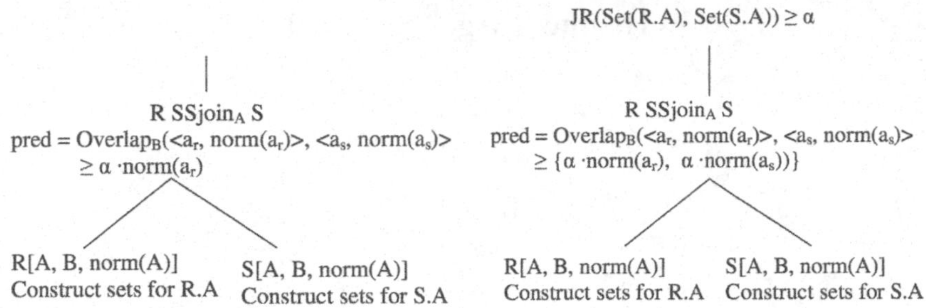

Figure 4.4: Jaccard containment and similarity joins.

As shown in Figure 4.1, let $R(OrgName, 3\quad gram, norm)$ and $S(OrgName, 3\quad gram, norm)$ associate the strings "Sweetlegal Investments" and "Sweeltegal Investment" with (1) the actual 3-grams in column $3\quad gram$, and (2) the number of 3-grams in column $norm$.

We can see that the jaccard containment predicate is equivalent to the following SSJoin predicate: $Overlap_B(\langle a, norm\rangle_r, \langle a, norm\rangle_s)\quad 0.8\quad R.norm$.

In general, we construct relations $R\langle A, B, norm(A)\rangle$ and $S\langle A, B, norm(A)\rangle$ from Rbase and Sbase respectively, that associates a string with (1) the weight of the underlying set, and (2) the set of elements in its underlying set. The jaccard containment condition can then be expressed using the operator tree shown in Figure 4.4. Note that because jaccard containment like the SSJoin operator measures the degree of overlap, this translation does not require a post-processing step.

Observe that for any two sets s_1 and s_2, $JC(s_1, s_2)\quad JR(s_1, s_2)$. Hence, $JR(s_1, s_2)$ $\phi \Rightarrow Max(JC(s_1, s_2), JC(s_2, s_1))\quad \phi$. Therefore, as shown on the right hand side in Figure 4.4, we use the operator tree for jaccard containment and add the check for jaccard similarity as a post-processing filter. In fact, we check for the jaccard containment of $JC(R.A, S.A)$ and $JC(S.A, R.A)$ being greater than ϕ.

4.3 IMPLEMENTING THE SSJOIN OPERATOR

In this section, we discuss the implementation of the SSJoin operator. We consider various strategies, each of which can be implemented using relational operators. The idea is to exploit the property that SSJoin has to only return pairs of groups whose similarity is above a certain threshold, and that thresholds are usually high. In this section, we talk mostly about executing the operation $R\ SSJoin_A^{pred}\ S$ over relations $R(A, B)$ and $S(A, B)$ where the predicate is $Overlap_B(a_r, a_s)\quad \phi$ for some positive constant ϕ. The implementation extends to the case when $Overlap_B(a_r, a_s)$ is required to be greater than a set of expressions.

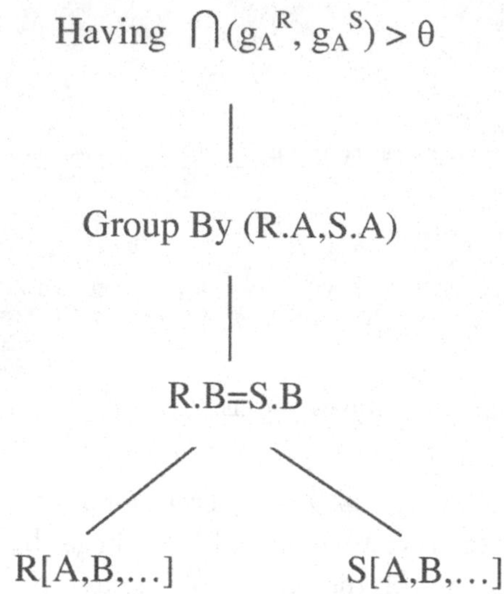

Figure 4.5: Basic implementation of SSJoin.

4.3.1 BASIC SSJOIN IMPLEMENTATION

Since $\phi > 0$, we can conclude that for a pair $<a_r, a_s>$ to be returned, at least one of the values in the column B related to a_r and a_s must be the same. Indeed, by computing an equi-join on the B column(s) between R and S and adding the weights of all joining values of B, we can compute the overlap between groups on $R.A$ and $S.A$. Figure 4.5 presents the operator tree for implementing the basic overlap-SSJoin. We first compute the equi-join between R and S on the join condition $R.B = S.B$. Any $\langle R.A, S.A\rangle$ pair whose overlap is non-zero would be present in the result. Grouping the result on $\langle R.A, S.A\rangle$ and ensuring, through the having clause, that the overlap is greater than the specified threshold ϕ would yield the result of the SSJoin.

The size of the equi-join on B varies widely with the joint-frequency distribution of B. Consider the case when the SSJoin operator is used to implement the jaccard similarity between strings. Here, the values in the attribute B represent tokens contained in strings. Certain tokens like "the" and "inc" can be extremely frequent in both R and S relations. In such scenarios, which occur often, the size of the equi-join on B is very large. The challenge, therefore, is to reduce the intermediate number of $\langle R.A, S.A\rangle$ groups compared. Next, we describe our approach to address this problem.

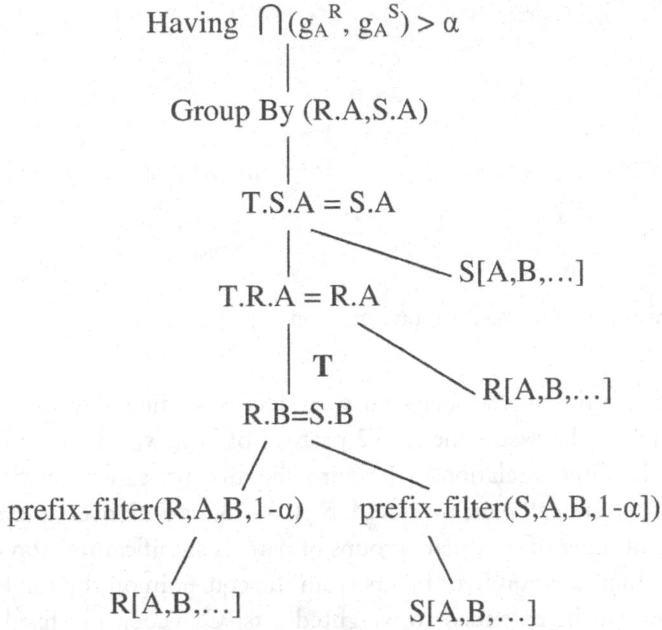

Figure 4.6: Prefix-filter implementation of SSJoin.

4.3.2 FILTERED SSJOIN IMPLEMENTATION

The intuition we exploit is that when two sets have a *large* overlap, even smaller subsets of the base sets overlap. To make the intuition concrete, consider the case when all sets are unweighted and have a fixed size h. We can observe the following property.

Property 4.9 Let s_1 and s_2 be two sets of size h. Consider any subset r_1 of s_1 of size $h \quad k + 1$. If $|s_1 \cap s_2| \quad k$, then $r_1 \cap s_2 \neq \sigma$.

For instance, consider the sets s_1={1,2,3,4,5} and s_2={1,2,3,4,6} which have an overlap of 4. Any subset of s_1 of size 2 has a non-zero overlap with the set s_2. Therefore, instead of performing an equi-join on R and S, we may ignore a large subset of S and perform the equi-join on R and a small filtered subset of S. By filtering out a large subset of S, we can reduce, often by very significant margins, the size of the resultant equi-join.

The natural question now is whether or not we can apply such a prefix-filter to both relations R and S in the equi-join. Interestingly, we find that the answer is in the affirmative. We illustrate this as follows. Fix an ordering $\mathcal{O}$ of the universe $\mathcal{U}$ from which all set elements are drawn. Define the k-prefix of any set s to be the subset consisting of the first k elements as per the ordering $\mathcal{O}$. Now, if $|s_1 \cap s_2| \quad k$, then their $(h \quad k + 1)$-prefixes must intersect. For example, consider $s_1 = \{1, 2, 3, 4, 5\}$ and $s_2 = \{1, 2, 3, 4, 6\}$ as before. Assume the usual ordering of

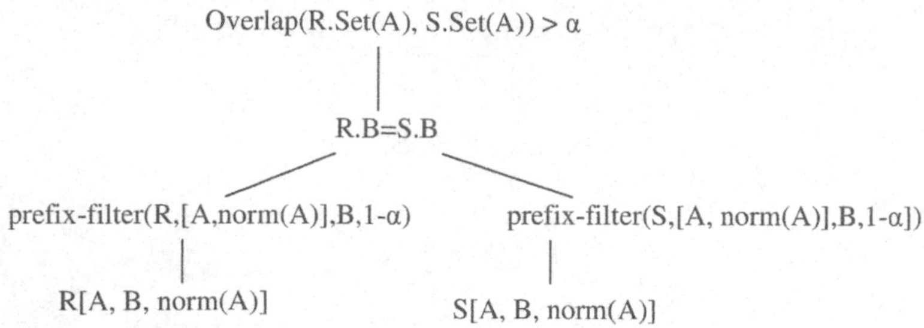

Figure 4.7: Prefix-filter with inline set representation.

natural numbers. Since the overlap between s_1 and s_2 is 4, their size $(5 \quad 4 + 1) = 2$-prefixes must intersect, which is the case—the size-2 prefixes of both s_1 and s_2 is $\{1, 2\}$. Therefore, an equi-join on B on the filtered relations will return all pairs that satisfy the SSJoin predicate. The result would be a superset of all pairs of $< R.A, S.A >$ groups with overlap greater than the given threshold. And the number of candidate groups of pairs is significantly (sometimes, by orders of magnitude) smaller than the number of pairs from the equi-join on the full base relations.

This intuition can be extended to weighted sets. Consider any fixed ordering O of the domain from which $R.B$ and $S.B$ are drawn. Given a weighted set r drawn from this domain, define *prefix* (r) to be the subset corresponding to the shortest prefix (in sorted order), the weights of whose elements add up to more than . We have the following result:

Lemma 4.10 Consider two weighted sets s_1 and s_2, such that $wt(s_1 \cap s_2) \quad \phi$. Let $\;_1 = wt(s_1) \quad \phi$ and $\;_2 = wt(s_2) \quad \phi$. Then $prefix_{\;1}(s_1) \cap prefix_{\;2}(s_2) \neq \sigma$.

Suppose that for the set defined by value $a_r \in R.A$, $Set(a_r)$ (respectively for $a_s \in S.A$), we extract a $\;_{a_r} = (wt(Set(a_r)) \quad \phi)$ prefix under $\mathcal{O}$ (respectively, a $\;_{a_s}$ prefix). From the above lemma, performing the equi-join B on the resulting relations will result in a superset of the result of the SSJoin. We can then check the SSJoin predicate on the pairs returned. Since the filter is letting only a prefix under a fixed order to pass through, we call this filter the *prefix-filter*. We refer to the relation obtained by filtering R as *prefix-filter*(R, ϕ).

The filtered overlap implementation of the SSJoin operator is illustrated in Figure 4.6. We first join the prefix-filtered relations to obtain candidate pairs $\langle R.A, S.A \rangle$ groups to be compared. We join the candidate set of pairs with the base relations R and S in order to obtain the groups so that we can compute the overlap between the groups. The actual computation of the overlap is done by grouping on $\langle R.A, S.A \rangle$ and filtering out groups whose overlap is less than ϕ.

We need to extend this implementation to address the following issues.

- *Normalized Overlap Predicates:* Instead of a constant ϕ as in the discussion above, if we have an expression of the form $\phi \quad R.Norm$, then we extract a $\;_{a_r, norm(a_r)} = (wt(Set(a_r)) \quad \phi$

$norm(a_r)$) prefix of the set $Set(a_r)$. This generalizes to the case when we have an expression involving constants and $R.Norm$.

- For a 2-sided normalized overlap predicate $Overlap_B(a_r, a_s) \geq \alpha \cdot Max(R.Norm, S.Norm)$, we apply different prefix-filter to relations R and S. We apply the filter *prefix-filter*$(R, \alpha \cdot R.Norm)$ to R and *prefix-filter*$(S, \alpha \cdot S.Norm)$ to S.

- For the evaluation of a 1-sided normalized overlap predicate $Overlap_B(a_r, a_s) \geq \alpha \cdot R.Norm$, we can apply the prefix-filter only on sets in R.

We also need to address the following issues for implementing the prefix-filter approach.

- **Mapping Multi-set Intersection to Joins**: Observe that the form of predicate we consider here involves multi-set intersection when any $R.A$ (or $S.A$) group contains multiple values on the $R.B$ attributes. In order to be able to implement them using standard relational operators, we convert these multi-sets into sets; we convert each value in $R.B$ and $S.B$ into an ordered pair containing an ordinal number to distinguish it from its duplicates. Thus, for example, the multi-set $\{1, 1, 2\}$ would be converted to $\{\langle 1, 1\rangle, \langle 1, 2\rangle, \langle 2, 1\rangle\}$. Since set intersections can be implemented using joins, the conversion enables us to perform multi-set intersections using joins.

- **Determining the Ordering**: Note that the prefix-filter is applicable no matter what ordering $\mathcal{O}$ we pick. The question arises whether the ordering picked can have performance implications. Clearly, the answer is that it does. Our goal is to pick an ordering that minimizes the number of comparisons that the ordering will imply. One natural candidate here is to order the elements by increasing order of their frequency in the database. This way, we try to eliminate higher frequency elements from the prefix filtering and thereby expect to minimize the number of comparisons. Since many common notions of weights (e.g., IDF) are inversely proportional to frequency, we can implement this using the element weights. Several optimization issues arise such as to what extent will prefix-filtering help, whether it is worth the cost of producing the filtered relations, whether we should proceed by partitioning the relations and using different approaches for different partitions, etc.

  We note that the following is a reasonably good choice: we order $R.B$ values with respect to their IDF weights. Since high frequency elements have lower weights, we filter them out first. Therefore, the size of the subset (and hence the subsequent join result) let through would be the smallest under this ordering.

- **Inlined Representation of Groups**: A property of the prefix-filter approach is that when we extract the prefix-filtered relations, we lose the original groups. Since the original groups are required for verifying the SSJoin predicate, we have to perform a join with the base relations again in order to retrieve the groups, as shown in Figure 4.6. These *retrieval* joins can clearly add substantially to the cost of the SSJoin operation.

Next, we discuss a new implementation which can avoid these retrieval joins. The idea is to "carry" the groups along with each $R.A$ and $S.A$ value that pass through the prefix-filter. This way, we can avoid the joins with the base relations. The intuition is illustrated in Figure 4.7. In order to do so, we either require the capability to define a set-valued attribute or a method to encode sets as strings or clobs, say by concatenating all elements together separating them by a special marker.

Now, measuring the overlap between $\langle R.A, S.A \rangle$ groups can be done without a join with the base relations. However, we require a function, say a UDF, for measuring overlap between inlined sets. This implementation goes beyond the capabilities of standard SQL operators as it requires us to compute set overlaps. However, the UDF we use is a simple unary operator that does not perform very sophisticated operations internally, especially when the sets are bounded. Hence, this alternative is usually more efficient than the prefix-filtered implementation since it avoids the redundant joins.

4.4 BIBLIOGRAPHY

Given the importance of the string similarity join for record matching, deduplication and other data cleaning tasks, the similarity join operation has received a lot of attention. The set similarity join abstraction, which is designed to support joins based on a variety of similarity functions, has been proposed by Chaudhuri et al. [2006b]. Some of the ideas for optimizing this join for particular similarity functions, such as edit distance and cosine similarity, have been discussed by Gravano et al. [2001], Sarawagi and Kirpal [2004], Bayardo et al. [2007], and Xiao et al. [2008]. Further optimizations on the implementation of the SSJoin operator have been proposed by Arasu et al. [2006]. A survey of several algorithms for performing similarity join have also been discussed in a survey by Koudas et al. [2006]. More recently, a parallel implementation of the set similarity join using the mapreduce framework has been developed by Vernica et al. [2010].

CHAPTER 5

Operator: Clustering

Recall that the goal of the deduplication task is to "group" records in a relation that represents the same entity. The grouping typically requires that the records in a group be closer to each other, especially to each other than to records in other groups. A custom deduplication task may require that other constraints beyond similarity be satisfied as well. However, closeness to each other by textual similarity is a critical predicate, which needs to be satisfied.

In this chapter, we discuss the *clustering* operator, which is useful for deduplication and other data cleaning tasks. Informally speaking, clustering refers to the operation of taking a set of items, and putting them into smaller groups based on "similarity." For example, a list of restaurants may be clustered based on similar cuisines, or based on their price, or some combination of price and cuisine.

We start by presenting formal definitions of clustering in Section 5.1, then present some common clustering techniques used in data cleaning in Section 5.2, and conclude with a brief bibliography in Section 5.3.

5.1 DEFINITIONS

We start with a generic definition of clustering to capture the general intuition behind clustering. We then progressively refine the definition to guide the solution toward a desirable solution.

Definition 5.1 Clustering. Given a set $S = \{I_1, \ldots, I_n\}$ of items, a clustering $\mathcal{C}$ of S is defined by a set of subsets $\mathcal{C} = \{C_1, \ldots, C_m\}$, where:

- each $C_j \subseteq S$
- $S = \bigcup_{j=1}^{m} C_j$
- for $i \neq j$, $C_i \neq C_j$

Each C_j is called a *cluster*.

Obviously the definition above is too generic to be useful by itself. Therefore, clustering tasks are guided by a *similarity measure*, sim, that is expressed in a pairwise fashion and gives the similarity between a pair of items.[1] Intuitively, the goal of clustering is to group S into multiple clusters $\{C_1, \ldots, C_m\}$, where each cluster C_j contains similar items based on the similarity

[1]Sometimes the input to clustering is a *distance measure*, instead of a similarity measure, which can be turned into a similarity measure.

measure sim. There are multiple ways in which the similarity measure may be used to guide the clustering process, and the "goodness" of clustering is often formally captured using an *objective function*:

Definition 5.2 Clustering Objective Function. Given a set $S = \{I_1, \ldots, I_n\}$ of items and a similarity measure $sim : S \times S \rightarrow [0, 1]$, a clustering objective function Obj is a function that associates a numeric value $Obj(\mathcal{C}, sim)$ to every clustering $\mathcal{C}$.

Intuitively, the goal is to find a clustering that optimizes the value of the objective function.

Example 5.3 One example of a clustering objective is based on the average intra-cluster similarity. We can define *cluster similarity* as the average pairwise similarity of all items in a cluster:

$$CSim(C_j, sim) = \mathbf{avg}_{I_p, I_q \in C_j} sim(I_p, I_q)$$

The clustering objective is then defined as the minimum cluster similarity among all clusters:

$$Obj(\mathcal{C}, sim) = \max_{C_j \in \mathcal{C}} CSim(C_j, sim)$$

Note that the objective function above is presented only as an example. However, just by itself the objective function may admit an extreme solution, such as creating n clusters, each consisting of a single item I_i since that would maximize the value of the objective above. Therefore, to be used in practice the objective function or clustering specification needs to be refined further. To avoid such extreme solutions, and optionally to encode domain knowledge, clustering is also frequently guided by a set of *constraints* that restricts the valid set of clusterings:

Definition 5.4 Clustering Constraint. Given a set $S = \{I_1, \ldots, I_n\}$ of items, a similarity measure $sim : S \times S \rightarrow [0, 1]$, a clustering constraint is a boolean function that returns *true* or *false* for any clustering $\mathcal{C}$ of S. Intuitively, a clustering is *valid* if all constraints imposed are satisfied (*true*), and invalid otherwise.

Example 5.5 One simple example of a constraint is to restrict the size of each cluster: we might want to restrict the clustering of a set of restaurants into clusters of between 5 and 10 restaurants. Or, given a set of images, we might want to cluster into exactly two clusters, grouping them into good/bad images. In more general cases, we may have complex *aggregate functions* based on attributes associated with each item and impose constraints on the aggregate value of attributes within each cluster.

A specific constraint that is often useful in data cleaning (and other tasks) is that of imposing disjointness among all clusters, i.e., each item can only belong to one cluster.

Definition 5.6 Disjoint Clustering. A clustering $\mathcal{C} = \{C_1, \ldots, C_m\}$ is said to be disjoint if $\forall 1 \le r < s \le m : (C_r \cap C_s) = \emptyset$.

Disjointness is particularly useful when future decisions on each cluster is made in an independent fashion, such as in deduplication tasks where each cluster may be operated on in a distributed fashion.

Example 5.7 Consider deduplicating a list of tennis players in a table that provides information on the number of grand slams won by each tennis player, as shown in Table 5.1.

Table 5.1: Table listing player names with number of grand slams won. The player names need to be deduplicated

Player Name	Grand Slams Won
R. Federer	13
D. Ferrer	4
Rafa Nadal	6
Rafael Nadal	3

Suppose our task is to deduplicate the player names, we can formulate a clustering problem as follows: Each resulting cluster would represent a distinct player. The pairwise similarity between records is given by the 3-grams jaccard string similarity we've seen in Chapter 3. We may also impose the following constraints: (1) Disjointness, since the same tuple in the table cannot represent two different people; (2) Suppose we know that no player has won more than 15 grand slam titles, we impose the constraint that the sum of grand slams won of all records in a given cluster is at most 15; (3) The average intra-cluster similarity must be at least 0.5. We may then solve the clustering with the objective of minimizing the number of clusters. We may then obtain the result as shown in Table 5.2. Note, however, if we didn't impose the second constraint above, we may have grouped "D. Ferrer" and "R. Federer" together if they have a string similarity greater than 0.5.

We shall later also study an important example of clustering in an operation called *blocking* as a pre-processing step in deduplication: intuitively, the set of all items to be deduplicated are divided into disjoint clusters, and fine-grained deduplication is performed only within each cluster.

Table 5.2: List of grouped tennis players obtained after deduplicating records from Table 5.1 based on the constraints in Example 5.7

Player ID	Names of Players
1	R. Federer
2	D. Ferrer
3	Rafa Nadal, Rafael Nadal

5.2 TECHNIQUES

Clustering is a very widely studied topic and many techniques have been proposed (see Section 5.3 for pointers to bibliography). In this section, we present a brief overview of some basic clustering techniques that are used in the context of data cleaning.

5.2.1 HASH PARTITION

One technique for clustering is to assign items to clusters based on a *hash function* defined over attributes of items. Intuitively, the hash function should be such that similar items (based on a similarity function sim) are more likely to be get the same hash value based on H. Each hash value then corresponds to a distinct cluster in the clustering. Suppose our goal is to cluster a set S of items, where each item is from a domain D. We define a hash function $H : D \rightarrow D_H$, with a finite domain D_H. We can then construct a clustering of items $S = \{I_1, \ldots, I_n\}$ as equivalence classes of hash values:

$$\forall h \in D_H : \text{ let } C(h) = \{I_i \in S | H(I_i) = h\}$$

Then, the clustering is defined as:

$$\mathcal{C} = \bigcup_{h \in D_H} \{C(h)\}$$

Example 5.8 In order to cluster a set of restaurants based on their expense, we can define a hash function that produces an integer value by dividing the average expense per person at the restaurant by 10, rounding to the nearest dollar. We can then use the process above and we will obtain a clustering where all restaurants are placed in clusters based on the following groups of average prices: [\$0, \$10], (\$10, \$20], and so on. (Note that strictly speaking the domain of hash values is infinite here, but for a given dataset of restaurants, we obtain a finite number of clusters.)

Note that the clustering process described above generated a disjoint clustering, and this is a common process used in blocking, which we shall study in Chapter 8.

Further, we can impose constraints on the clustering by incorporating constraints on the hash function. The following example shows how to impose a restriction on the number of clusters.

Example 5.9 If we have a constraint that the number of clusters must be at most 4, we can revise the hash function from above and define the hash function to produce four possible values based on the average prices being in ranges of say $[0, 20]$, $(20, 40]$, $(40, 100]$, $(100, \infty)$.

Imposing a constraint on the size of clusters in a hash-based clustering is a little trickier, but doable as illustrated by the example below.

Example 5.10 Continuing with the restaurants example, if we want to restrict the size of each cluster to at most 100 restaurants, we may start with one specific clustering, and iteratively "split" large clusters. For instance, if all clusters except the one corresponding to $[0, 10]$ are under the size of 100. We may create a finer partition of the average price to the ranges $[0, 5]$, $(5, 10]$, and if needed refine further. In this fashion we can "drill-down" the hash function until the size constraint is met.[2]

Finally, we can also extend the hash-based partitioning discussed above to obtain non-disjoint clusters if desired. We may use a family of hash functions and place items in clusters based on each of the hash values. In such a case, each cluster will be placed in K clusters, where K is the number of hash functions being used. In the blocking process, we often want to use multiple hash functions so that if two records are similar, they will match on at least one hash value. For example, we can preprocess a large set of restaurants by creating (non-disjoint) clustering based on hash functions on each of price, cuisine, location, name. We are then likely to catch most duplicates by a pairwise comparison within each cluster, assuming all duplicates have a matching hash value on at least one of the above attributes. We shall discuss this process further in Chapter 8.

5.2.2 GRAPH-BASED CLUSTERING

Next we briefly present clustering techniques, based on picturing the set of items in the form of a graph, which are useful for deduplication. The set of items $S = \{I_1, \ldots, I_n\}$ form the nodes of our graph, and there is a weighted edge between nodes I_i and I_j with weight given by the pairwise similarity $sim(I_i, I_j)$. The first step in clustering is to *threshold* the graph above, by only retaining edges whose weight is above some threshold τ. Let the resultant graph be denoted $G(V, E)$, where V corresponds to items in I, and E is the set of unweighted edges such that $(I_i, I_j) \in E$ if and only if $sim(I_i, I_j) \geq \tau$. We can now cluster the set S using standard graph clustering techniques such as:

[2] A minor point is that if there are more than 100 restaurants with an identical price, we will either violate the constraint, or need to arbitrarily split the cluster into smaller ones.

Connected Components: Compute all *connected components* of G, with each connected component forming a cluster. Note that we obtain disjoint clustering using this approach.

Cliques: Compute all *maximum cliques* of G, and each maximum clique forms a cluster. Note that here we may obtain non-disjoint clusters, as maximal cliques of a graph G are not necessarily disjoint.

In both the mechanisms above, or in other graph-based algorithm, we may choose to optionally impose constraints. As an example, if there is a constraint on the maximum number of clusters, we may choose to combine multiple connected components (or equivalently, lower the threshold τ) so as to obtain fewer clusters.

5.3 BILBIOGRAPHY

Clustering is a very widely studied topic in various domains, and therefore, it is impractical to present a comprehensive bibliography of clustering. Instead, we refer the reader to the book by Han and Kamber [2006] as well as to the Wikipedia article (http://en.wikipedia.org/wiki/Cluster_analysis), which provides a great taxonomy of clustering approaches. A detailed study of hash-based clustering, one of the approaches we discussed earlier, was the subject of Das Sarma et al. [2012]. Our focus in this chapter was to synthesize the basic approaches of clustering as applicable to data cleaning.

CHAPTER 6

Operator: Parsing

In this chapter, we discuss the *parsing* operator for segmenting an input string into its constituent attribute values. Recall that the task of inserting new records into a target data warehouse often requires the reconciliation of schema of the input records and that of the target records. The process of reconciliation would often involve "segmenting" a column of an input record into multiple target columns. The segmented input records may then be compared and, if needed, inserted into the target table. We now discuss an example to illustrate the goal, and the challenges. Revisiting our earlier example, an input address string "15633 148th Ave Bellevue WA 98004" has to be split into the following sub-components before populating a destination customer address table:

House Number: `15633`
Street Name: `148th Ave.`
City: `Bellevue`
State: `WA` **Zip:** `98004`

A similar requirement arises in product databases where a product description has to be parsed into sub-components involving specification of the product's attributes. For example, "Canon EOS Rebel T3i 18-55 mm IS II Kit" has to be segmented as follows.

Brand: `Canon`
Model: `EOS Rebel T3i`
Lens: `18-55 mm`
Modifier: `IS II Kit`

In general, the goal of a *parsing* operator is to split an incoming string into segments each of which may be inserted as attribute values at the target. The following definition formalizes the goal of the parsing operator.

Definition 6.1 Parsing. Given a string T and a relational schema $\mathcal{S} = \{A_1, \ldots, A_n\}$, construct a tuple t with schema $\mathcal{S}$ from T.

The main technical challenge is to identify the points in the input string that define its segments, and to assign the segments to attributes in the target schema so that each segment is a valid attribute value.

An alternative *attribute extraction* formulation is to allow fragments of the input string to be ignored, and view this problem as extracting fragments from the input to fill in attribute values. In the example string involving Canon camera, the extraction of the attribute Modifier may not be required, and this particular fragment could be ignored. It is conceivable to modify the segmentation formulation to insert extraneous attributes between real attributes in order to consume unimportant fragments. A formulation of this generalization has been extensively explored in the context of information extraction. In the following, we only focus on the parsing formulation.

6.1 REGULAR EXPRESSIONS

One approach we can adopt is to use regular expressions to achieve the desired segmentation. For example, consider the regular expression:

```
(\d*) (.*[a|A]ve[.]) (.*), ([A-Z][A-Z]) (\d\d\d\d\d)
```

The expression above would accept the string "18100 New Hamshire Ave. Silver Spring, MD 20861." The segment of the string accepted by each group (within parenthesis) defines an attribute value. Notice that we would have to develop many such regular expressions to deal with the variety of addresses that may be used in USA (e.g., allow street names, states to be completely spelled out, zipcode to include the 4-digit extension). The development would require deep domain expertise as well as the ability to correctly develop such regular expressions. When we expand the domain of addresses to be beyond USA, then the task of specifying regular expressions for segmentation becomes significantly more complex.

Let us consider the string "18100 New Hamshire, Silver Spring, MD 20861" where the token "Ave" is missing the street name attribute value. The above example regular expression cannot accept this input string, since it is not robust to tolerate errors in the input. We can try to make the regular expression more general and robust to tolerate such input errors. For example, the following modified regular expression is a candidate:

```
(\d*) (.*[\.]) (.*), ([A-Z][A-Z]) (\d\d\d\d\d)
```

Making regular expressions tolerant to errors adds significant complexity to the development task. To deal with errors, we would have to add more general regular expressions along with specific ones, which accept correctly specified input.

A consequence of having a large set of regular expressions is that an input string may be accepted by many regular expressions. Further, each of them may result in a different segmentation and attribute value assignment. Which one of these is the correct or the most likely to be correct segmentation? This particular challenge of choosing the optimal segmentation is not easily solved by the use of regular expressions.

6.2 HIDDEN MARKOV MODELS

Based on the challenges observed above, we essentially require a mechanism to "score" a segmentation of an input string. This is effectively addressed by the use of ***hidden markov models (HMMs)***.

Intuitively, HMMs encode a set of regular expressions along with the score associated with a regular expression accepting an attribute value. A regular expression that is more indicative of an attribute value will have a higher score than one that is generic and can accept values from different attributes. Further, HMMs enable efficiently identifying the "best scoring" segmentation among all acceptable segmentations. We first briefly summarize HMMs before discussing how we can use HMMs for parsing.

An HMM is a probabilistic finite state automaton which encodes the probability distribution of sequences of symbols, each drawn from a finite input dictionary. Given a sequence s of input symbols, we can compute the probability of observing s. A HMM comprises a set of states and a dictionary of output symbols. Each state can emit symbols from the output dictionary with different probabilities per symbol. States are connected by directed edges which encode possible *transitions* between states. There are two special states: a *start* state and an *end* state. Beginning from the start state, a HMM generates an output sequence $O = o_1, \ldots, o_k$ by making k transitions from one state to the next until the end state is reached. The ith symbol o_i is generated by the ith transition in the path based on that state's probability distribution of the dictionary symbols. In general, an output sequence can be generated through multiple paths each with some probability. The sum of these probabilities is the total probability with which the HMM generates the output sequence. Thus, the HMM induces a probability distribution on sequences of symbols chosen from a discrete dictionary.

There are two primary issues that we need to address. First, how does one build appropriate HMMs for custom domains? Second, how do we use them to segment input strings? We now discuss these two issues.

6.2.1 TRAINING HMMS

A HMM model consists of a structural component defining the set of states and the possible transitions. The second component defines the emission and transition probabilities over the predetermined structure. Informally, a HMM model consists of

- a set of n states
- a dictionary of m output symbols
- an $n \times n$ *edge transition* matrix A where the ij^{th} element a_{ij} is the probability of making a transition from state i to state j, and
- a $n \times m$ *emission matrix* B where entry b_{jk} denotes the probability of emitting the kth output symbol in state j.

The training of an HMM has two phases. In the first phase we choose the structure of the HMM, that is, the number of states n and edges amongst states and train the dictionary. In the second phase we learn the transition and emission probabilities assuming a fixed structure of the HMM.

Structural Components

In general, a good structure of the HMM depends on the problem and the domain it is supposed to be applied upon. There are two typical approaches. The first *unified* approach relies on one HMM for parsing all attribute values. The second *hierarchical* approach first determines the order among attribute values in a given string, and then extracts fragments of each attribute value.

We first illustrate an example HMM structure for the unified approach. Figure 6.1 illustrates the structure of such an HMM for parsing attribute values from an address string.

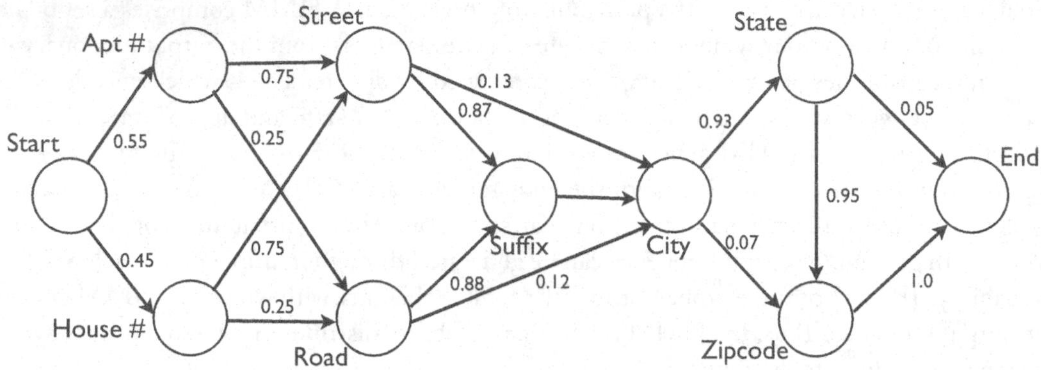

Figure 6.1: A unified HMM model for parsing addresses.

A common limitation of the unified approach is that the single HMM has to be cognizant of the structure (order and patterns of tokens) among attribute values as well as that within each attribute value. This sometimes is hard if token patterns across attribute values overlap. The following hierarchical approach addresses this issue.

The hierarchical approach adopts a two-level model, as shown in Figure 6.2. The higher level model decides on the ordering, probabilistically, among individual attributes. We have one lower level model per attribute, and each of them decides the best fragment of the input string that belongs to the attribute.

Outer HMM: The outer HMM has as many states as the number of attributes. The transitions between states reflect the probabilistic ordering expected among attributes in the input strings.

For learning the outer HMM, the training data is treated as a set of sequences of attribute values, ignoring the inner details of each attribute value. These sequences are then used to learn the outer HMM.

Inner HMM: We have several choices to decide from for the inner HMM's structure of each attribute. We illustrate a general class of such inner HMMs.

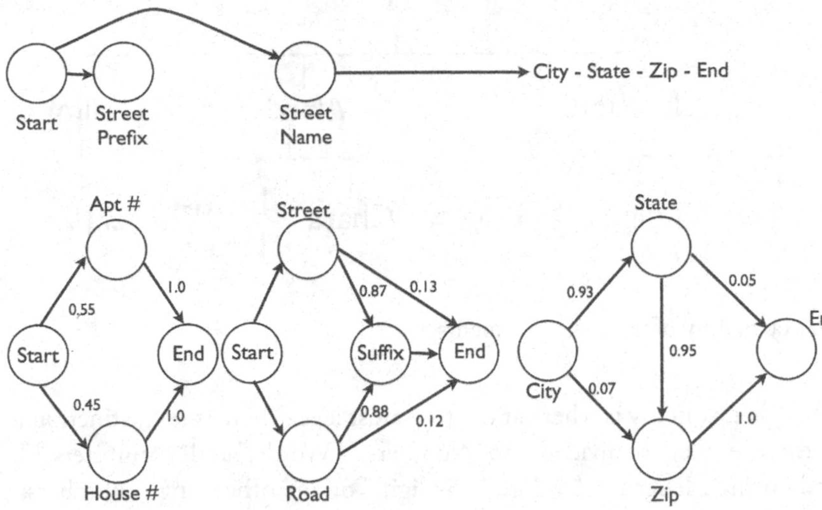

Figure 6.2: A hierarchical HMM model for parsing addresses.

Each inner HMM has a *start* and an *end* state. For a given value of k(1) there are k independent paths between the start and end states. For each i, (1 i k) there is a path with exactly i states between the start and the end states. The intuition is that a path with i states would capture the characteristics of attribute values with i tokens. All values with more k tokens would be captured by the path with k states—the last state has a transition to itself besides to the end state. Deciding on the correct value of k is dependent on the domain, and could be done experimentally.

An extreme instance of this structure is one where $k = 1$. That is, each inner HMM consists of a chain of *start*, *middle*, and *end* states with the following transitions: start to middle, middle to middle, and middle to end.

Taxonomy on dictionary elements: We have discussed the structure of the HMMs. One issue during the training phase is what constitutes the symbols in the dictionary. A reasonable approach is to treat each distinct word, number, or delimiter in the training data as a token. Thus, in the address 18100 New Hampshire Ave. Silver Spring, MD 20861 we have 10 tokens: six words, two numbers, and two delimiters "," and ".". Intuitively, though we expect the specific number "18100" to be unimportant as far as we know that it is a number and not a word. Similarly, for the zip code field the specific value "20816" is not important; what matters perhaps is that it is a 5-digit number.

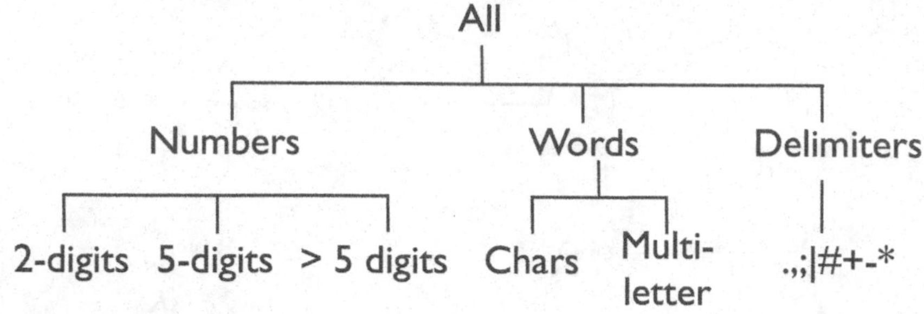

Figure 6.3: A taxonomy of dictionary elements.

An example taxonomy is where at the top-most level, there is no distinction amongst symbols; at the next level they are divided into "Numbers," "Words," and "Delimiters;" "Numbers" are divided based on their length as "3-digit," "5-digit," or any other length numbers; and so on. A more generalized taxonomy is shown in Figure 6.3. Here, all numbers are generalized to a single special token representing numbers. All delimiters are generalized to another special symbol.

Learning Probabilities

The goal of the probability learning process is to learn matrices A and B such that the probability of the HMM generating these training sequences is maximized. Each training sequence consists of a series of element-symbol pairs. The structure of the HMM is fixed and each state is marked with one of the E elements. This restricts the states to which the symbols of a training sequence can be mapped. The transition probabilities can be calculated using the Maximum Likelihood approach on all training sequences. Accordingly, the probability of making a transition from state i to state j is the ratio of the number of transitions made from state i to state j in the training data to the total number of transitions made from state i. This can be written as:

$$a_{ij} = \frac{\text{Number of transitions from state i to state j}}{\text{Total number of transitions out of state i}} \tag{6.1}$$

The emission probabilities are computed similarly. The probability of emitting symbol k in state j is the ratio of the number of times symbol k was emitted in state j to the total number of symbols emitted in the state. This can be written as:

$$b_{jk} = \frac{\text{Number of times the k-th symbol emitted at state j}}{\text{Total number of symbols emitted at state j}} \tag{6.2}$$

Computationally, training the A and B matrix involves making a single pass over all input training sequences, mapping each sequence to its unique path in the HMM and adding up the counts for each transition that it makes and output symbol it generates.

The above formula for emission probabilities needs to be refined when the training data is insufficient. Often during testing we encounter words that have not been seen during training. The above formula will assign a probability of zero for such symbols causing the final probability to be zero irrespective of the probability values elsewhere in the path. Hence assigning a correct probability to the unknown words is important. The traditional method for smoothing is Laplace smoothing according to which Equation 6.2 will be modified to add one to the numerator and m to the denominator. Thus, an unseen symbol k, in state j will be assigned probability $\frac{1}{T_j+m}$ where T_j is the denominator of Equation 6.2 and stands for the total number of tokens seen in state j.

A potentially better alternative is based on the following intuition. An element like "road name," that during training has seen more distinct words than an element like "Country," is expected to also encounter unseen symbols more frequently during testing. Laplace smoothing does not capture this intuition. We use a method called absolute discounting. In this method we subtract a small value, say x from the probability of all known m_j distinct words seen in state j. We then distribute the accumulated probability equality amongst all unknown values. Thus, the probability of an unknown symbol is $\frac{m_j x}{m-m_j}$ and for a known symbol k is $b_{jk} - x$ where b_{jk} is as calculated in Equation 6.2. There is no theory about how to choose the best value of x, but we may x as $\frac{1}{T_j+m}$.

6.2.2 USE OF HMMS FOR PARSING

We now discuss how HMMs are used to actually segment an input string. Given an output symbol sequence $O = o_1, o_2, \ldots, o_k$, we want to associate each symbol with a state in the HMM—the state that emitted the symbol. Hence we need to find a path of length k from the start state to the end state, such that the ith symbol o_i is emitted by the ith state in the path. In general, an output sequence can be generated through multiple paths, each with some probability. We assume the Viterbi approximation and say that the path having the highest probability is the one which generated the output sequence. Given n states and a sequence of length k, there can be $O(k^n)$ possible paths that the sequence can go through. This exponential complexity is cut down to $O(kn^2)$ by the famous dynamic programming-based Viterbi Algorithm. We now discuss the Viterbi algorithm.

The Viterbi algorithm

Given an output sequence $O = o_1, o_2, \ldots, o_k$ of length k and an HMM having n states, we want to find out the most probable state sequence from the start state to the end state which generates O. Let 0 and $n + 1$ denote the special start and end states. Let $v_s(i)$ be the probability of the most probable path for the prefix $o_1, o_2, \ldots, o_i$ of O that ends with state s. We begin at the start state labeled 0. Thus, initially

$$v_0(0) = 1, v_k(0) = 0, k \neq 0$$

Subsequent values are found using the following recursive formulation:

$$v_s(i) = b_s(o_i)\ max_{1 \le r \le n}\{a_{rs} v_r(i-1)\},\ 1 \le s \le n,\ 1 \le i \le k$$

where $b_s(o_i)$ is the probability of emitting the ith symbol o_i at state s and a_{rs} is the transition probability from state r to state s. The maximum is taken over all states of the HMM.

The probability of the most probable path that generates the output sequence O is given by the following equation.

$$v_{n+1} = max_{1 \le r \le n} a_{r(n+1)} v_r(k)$$

The actual path can be found by storing the argmax at each step. This formulation can be implemented as a dynamic programming algorithm running in $O(kn^2)$ time.

6.3 BIBLIOGRAPHY

The use of regular expressions for segmenting and extracting sub-strings which exhibit certain known patterns has been a common practice for many years. As mentioned earlier, this approach requires deep understanding of the patterns in the domain, and could also be brittle if the input contains small errors. The problem of segmentation has been formalized by Borkar et al. [2001], which also introduced the use of Markov models for robustly segmenting input records into target schema. The problem of segmenting input strings into records is closely related to that of *information extraction*, where the broad goal is to extract records of information from text documents. Many approaches, such as rule-based extraction [Chiticariu et al., 2010], Markov models [Mccallum and Freitag, 2000], relational learning [Califf and Mooney, 1999], and conditional random fields [Sarawagi and Cohen, 2004], have been applied to address this problem.

CHAPTER 7

Task: Record Matching

We discuss the record matching task in this chapter. Recall that the goal of record matching is to ascertain whether records across two relations represent the same real-world entity, often referred to as "matching." This important task needs to be solved while importing new customer sales records into the customer relation in a data warehouse. The customer records in the incoming sales need to be matched with existing customers to avoid subsequent issues with duplicating the same customer across multiple records. In the comparison shopping scenario, matching offers on products with the master catalog of products also requires matching the product referred to in the offer with the master catalog's product. Further, the record matching task may have to be solved while deduping records (say, customers or products) in a particular relation. While record matching may be formally defined in multiple ways, below we present a commonly used abstraction:

Definition 7.1 Record Matching. Given a relation $R(ID_R, A_1, \ldots, A_n)$ and $S(ID_S, B_1, \ldots, B_m)$ where ID is a key of each of the relations, construct a relation $Matches(ID_R, ID_S) \subseteq (\pi_{ID_R}(R) \times \pi_{ID_S}(S))$ such that for any $r \in R, s \in S$, $(r.ID_R, s) \in Matches(ID_R, ID_S)$ iff r and s represent the same real-world entity.

Naturally, it is not always possible to obtain $Matches$ exactly without human curation; therefore, the quality of any record matching result is generally measured empirically using standard *precision*, *recall* metrics. As described above, record matching poses two major challenges: (1) Given a pair (r, s) of tuples, $r \in R$ and $s \in S$, how do we determine whether to include (r, s) in $Matches$. Typically, this is done using a *similarity measure* sim, which assigns a numeric score $sim(r, s) \in [0, 1]$ to a pair, and then we may include all pairs with $sim(r, s) > \tau$ for some threshold τ. (2) Since relations R and S may be very large, a second challenge is that of pruning the number of pairs (r, s) for which to invoke the similarity measure. One option is to rely on hashing (possibly multiple times) records from R and S into buckets based on their attribute values, and only comparing pairs of records within buckets. Another option, when applicable, is to rely on the set similarity join to efficiently determine pairs of similar records from R and S. In general, record matching is applied to relations R and S, where the individual relations don't contain any duplicates; we describe a separate process to eliminate duplicates from one relation in Chapter 8.

Record matching is usually performed after schema matching, which ensures that the attributes in the two relations have been aligned. We start by discussing Schema Matching (in

Section 7.1). Then, we study record matching assuming R and S have the same schema (in Section 7.2); in other words, Section 7.2 assumes that the two input datasets have been converted to one single format.

7.1 SCHEMA MATCHING

Schema matching is the process of aligning schemas between multiple relations. While there are multiple formulations of schema matching, we focus on the specific version of schema matching that is relevant for the overall task of record matching: Given a relation $S(B_1, \ldots, B_m)$, obtain a *mapping* of S to a relation $R(A_1, \ldots, A_m)$. As an example, we may want to populate tuples from $S(Company, Apt, Street, City, Zip, Nation, PhoneNumber)$ into relation $R(Name, CityAddress, Country, Phone)$. Broadly, this task involves two challenges: (1) The first challenge is in determining *attribute correspondences* between the two relations, capturing which pairs of attributes in S and R refer to similar concepts. For example, we would like attribute correspondences $(Company, Name)$, $(Apt, CityAddress)$, $(Street, CityAddress)$, $(City, CityAddress)$, $(Nation, Country)$, and so on. (2) The second challenge is to use the attribute correspondences and compose them to obtain a function to convert tuples of S into tuples of R. For example, this would involve determining that the $CityAddress$ in R is obtained from an S tuple by concatenating the Apt, $Street$, and $City$, or that the $Phone$ in R is obtained by directly taking the $PhoneNumber$ from S. The first subtask above is usually referred to as *schema matching* while the second task is referred to as *schema mapping*. We confine our attention to matching in this book, which is performed using a (semi-)automatic process. Once a matching (or candidate matchings) are obtained, a programmer inspects the matchings, constructs a mapping, and implements it to convert S into R's format.

Attribute correspondences between R and S are obtained by considering every pair of attributes and computing a *similarity* or *relatedness* score. Then, pairs with a high score are retained. The similarity score between a pair of attributes, say B_i and A_j, are typically obtained by combining multiple signals such as those enumerated below:

- **Attribute Name:** We consider the similarity of the names of the attributes, by using a distance string distance measure from Chapter 3. Using similarity of attribute names enables us to detect correspondences such as $(Phone, PhoneNumber)$, but does not enable us to capture similar concepts with completely different names, such as $Country$ and $Nation$.

- **Attribute Values:** The next signal looks at the overlap in the set of values of the pair of attributes in the two relations. For example, if the string values in the $Country$ and $Nation$ column are similar, we may infer that they refer to the same concept. For similarity in the set of values, we may use a similarity measure such as jaccard similarity. In some cases, we may choose to apply some *set expansion* technique to enumerate a larger list of values before applying jaccard similarity. For example, if a column has 15 countries, and we recognize them to be countries, we could expand the list to all countries. Set expansion would ensure that even if the values from the two attributes don't have high overlap since each of them list only a few distinct countries, the expanded sets are very similar.

- **Attribute Labels:** The next signal considers looking at any known *labels* or *annotations* on the two relations' attributes. If the relations are obtained from webpages or text documents, looking at the context around the relation, and values in the table, we may be able to obtain class labels on a column. For instance, by observing names of people in a column, we may infer that an attribute refers to a *person* and assign the person label. We can use similarity in labels as another signal; sometimes, labels may not be identical, e.g., *company* versus *IT company*, in which case we must consider the relatedness of the labels.

- **Co-occurrence:** Co-occurrence of attribute names can provide a helpful signal in cases where a pair of attributes refers to the same concept but has completely different names. We can use the probabilities of other strings appearing together with attributes B_i and A_j as a way of computing the similarity between B_i and A_j. For example, we may infer the similarity of $Nation$ and $Country$ by combining the faces that: (1) the likelihood of attributes such as $Population$, $Capital$, etc., appearing in a relation that contains $Country$ is roughly the same as the likelihood of the attributes appearing in a relation that contains $Nation$; (2) $Country$ and $Nation$ co-occur in a relation very rarely. Obviously, using the signal above requires gathering statistics ahead of time using a large corpus of schemas.

- **Functional Dependencies:** We may use the knowledge of functional dependencies in measuring the similarity of non-key attributes. For instance, suppose we know that $Company$ and $Name$ correspond to each other and are keys of the relations S and R respectively. We then know that if attributes B_i and A_j must match, then whenever the $Company/Name$ values of a tuple in S and R are the same, then their corresponding B_i/A_j values must be similar. For instance, S and R must list the same phone number (or similar, if the formats of the phone numbers are slightly different) for the same company (assuming there is a single phone number per company).

Schema matching can be an easy task for well-formed and similar relations, or be an extremely difficult task for very different and/or poorly structured relations; therefore, in many cases, signals such as those enumerated above are used as user-guidance, while the final schema matching is performed by a human who understands the two relations. Automatic generation of similarities speeds up the process by minimizing the amount of human input required.

7.2 RECORD MATCHING

Next we present a high-level abstraction that is useful in thinking of the record matching problem: Given relations R and S, our goal is to find pairs of records from R and S that correspond to the same real-world entity. We can convert an instance of the record matching problem into an instance of a bipartite graph matching problem. We show the main steps in this graph construction in Section 7.2.1. We then describe the process of generating weighted edges in Section 7.2.2, and describe how to solve the graph matching problem (and thereby the record matching problem) in Section 7.2.3.

7.2.1 BIPARTITE GRAPH CONSTRUCTION

Given an instance of the record matching problem with relations $R(ID_R, A_1, \ldots, A_n)$ and $S(ID_S, A_1, \ldots, A_n)$,[1] we construct a weighted bipartite graph $G(V_R, V_S, E \subseteq V_R \times V_S, W)$ where $V_R = \{I \mid \exists r \in R, r.ID = I\}$ and $V_S = \{I \mid \exists s \in S, s.ID = I\}$. In other words, V_R has a vertex corresponding to each tuple in R, and V_S has a vertex corresponding to each tuple in S. Further, there is a weight function $W : E \rightarrow [0, 1]$, which assigns weights for edges between one vertex in V_R and one vertex in V_S. Since there are no edges with both endpoints in V_R or both endpoints in V_S, G constitutes a bipartite graph. Also, the weights of all edges need not be materialized, and E may be a proper subset of $V_R \times V_S$; we shall see later that only edges with high weight are important for record matching.

Before demonstrating the connection between the bipartite graph and record matching, we present the definition of *graph matching*, a well-studied notion in graph theory: A graph matching $M \subseteq E$ for the graph $G(V_R, V_S, E, W)$ is any subset of edges that don't share an endpoint: If $(i_{r1}, i_{s1}), (i_{r2}, i_{s2}) \in M$, then $r_1 \neq r_2$ and $s_1 \neq s_2$.

We shall now see the connection between record matching and the graph G: Every record matching result corresponds to a graph matching in G, and every graph matching in G corresponds to a record matching result. Recall that we assume that individual relations R and S don't contain any duplicates. Therefore, the output $Matches(ID_R, ID_S) \subseteq (\pi_{ID_R}(R) \times \pi_{ID_S}(S))$ of record matching satisfies the property that a specific ID_R value, say i_r, can appear with at most one ID_S value: If $(i_r, i_{s1}), (i_r, i_{s2}) \in Matches(ID_R, ID_S)$, then $s1 = s2$. Conversely, if $(i_{r1}, i_s), (i_{r2}, i_s) \in Matches(ID_R, ID_S)$, then $r1 = r2$. Therefore, every record matching result $Matches(ID_R, ID_S)$ in fact corresponds to a graph matching M in G, and every graph matching result M in G corresponds to a record matching result $Matches(ID_R, ID_S)$. Therefore, record matching can be reduced to the graph matching problem. Next we shall see how to construct the set of edges in G, followed by a solution to the graph matching problem.

7.2.2 WEIGHTED EDGES

We need to address two challenges in construction of the weighted edges in the graph $G(V_R, V_S, E \subseteq V_R \times V_S, W)$: (1) Determining E, the set of edges for which we want to associate a weight; (2) Determining the weight of the set of edges in E.

The first challenge above is relevant if the input relations R and S are very large, in which case naively set $E = V_R \times V_S$ can be very expensive. Intuitively, we want to retain all edges that potentially correspond to a record matching; therefore, we would like to have an edge $(r.ID, s.ID)$ in E if r and s are likely to be the same real-world entity. One approach is to consider a tuple

[1]Note we use the same set of attributes for R and S now since we assume the same schema for the relations.

r, and perform a "nearest neighbor search" in S to obtain all *candidate tuples* in S that we would like to form an edge with. Specifically, we could use the intuition that for a tuple r to match a tuple s in S, it is very likely that at least one attribute value is shared by the two tuples. Therefore, given a tuple r, we can consider all tuples in S that share at least one attribute's value with r to form edges in E; these candidates in S can be looked up by means of an index. Conversely, we could use a tuple s in S, and look up all tuples in R that share at least one attribute's value in R. Effectively, the constructions described above are obtained using the similarity join operator described in Chapter 4.

The second challenge described above, that of obtaining weights on edges, is arguably a significantly harder problem. Given a pair of tuples (r, s), our goal is to obtain a weight in [0, 1] that represents the similarity between the tuples; the higher the weight, the more likely it is that r and s match. The basic idea used is to generate weights is: (1) generate a set of *features*, corresponding to similarity in various attributes, and (2) combining the scores of all the features.

Features: For instance, given the relations R and S with the attributes in their schemas being $(A_1, \ldots, A_n)$, we consider features that correspond to the similarity in values of each of the attributes. The similarity measures used may be any of the measures described in Chapter 3, and we may apply multiple similarity measures on an attribute if desired. For example, we may use edit distance for an *address* attribute, or a numerical distance on some *age* attribute of a person, or the *budget* of a movie. A more sophisticated similarity measure may involve a jaccard similarity over set-valued attributes, such as the *genre* of movies. We need to exercise caution in the similarity measure for numerical attributes since the two relations may represent data in different units. For example, one relation represents the budget in dollars while another represents it in millions of dollars; in such cases, we would need to convert the data into the same unit and then apply the similarity measure.

In addition to standard similarity measures, we may want to generate customized features for a given domain or pair of relations. For instance, we want to apply *transformations* allowing the string "Bob" to be equated with "Robert" if they appear in a name attribute. We may also know that some parts of a string attribute are more important than another, the index at the end of a movie name (representing the sequel number), and give it a high weight in a modified edit distance computation.

Combining Features: Once the set of features is designed, for a pair of tuples (r, s), we obtain a *feature vector* $\bar{v} = \{v_1, \ldots, v_m\}$ corresponding to all the feature values for the pair of tuples. Our next goal is to combine these into a single weight value. Broadly speaking, there are two high-level ways to go about constructing a combination function: (1) Manually generated, hand-tuned combiner; (2) Machine-learned combination. In the first approach, a human who understands the domain of interest and the data in the two relations generates a combination function. An example of a combination function is the weighted average of all the feature values, where the weights can be hand-tuned based on the importance of attributes. The second approach is to use machine-learning, which requires a *training dataset* giving examples of pairs of tuples that are and are not real matches. Based on these known matches and non-matches, we can use machine-learning to learn a model of how to combine various features. Some commonly used models are SVMs, and binary decision trees. Note that these models can be used to give a binary output (equivalent to weights of 0 and 1), or a score in the range [0, 1].

7.2.3 GRAPH MATCHING

The final step in the record matching process is to perform graph matching on the constructed weighted bipartite graph. The main challenges in the graph matching problem are twofold: (1) determining which edges in the graph to retain as actual matches, (2) resolving conflicts among the retained edges to ensure the resulting set of edges constitutes a matching, i.e., no two edges share an endpoint.

The first challenge above is typically solved by applying a *threshold* τ on the edges, and retaining only edges with weights above τ. Obviously, the choice of τ is tricky and is either set by a human, or again picked by the machine based on some training examples. A higher τ generally ensures higher precision (at the cost of lower recall), while a lower τ generally increases recall (at the cost of lower precision); therefore, the choice of τ is determined by how much importance we want to give to precision and recall.

Once the threshold is applied, we are left with a set of edges E^t. If these edges represent a matching, we return them as the record matching result. However, if they aren't a matching, i.e., some edges share endpoints, we need to reduce the set of edges to a matching. Ideally, we would like to remove as few edges as possible (with as little weight as possible) from E^t to make it a matching. In other words, we want to retain a subset $E^s \subseteq E^t$ such that: (1) E^s is a matching, (2) the total weight of all edges in E^s is as high as possible. This problem is a classical graph theory problem known as the *max. weight matching* problem. Therefore, we use known max. weight matching techniques to obtain E^s and return the result.

7.3 BIBLIOGRAPHY

The study of record matching dates all the way back to over 50 years to the seminal pieces of work by Fellegi and Sunter [1969], Newcombe et al. [1959]. The problem continued to receive attention in the literature of late with the focus on maintaining data quality in data warehouses. Two more recent surveys discuss a set of topics relevant to record matching. The first one focuses on similarity measures for record matching [Koudas et al., 2006], while the second covers string similarity measures [Cohen et al., 2003]. Finally, see a recent study of record matching techniques are discussed by Christen [2012a].

CHAPTER 8

Task: Deduplication

In this chapter, we discuss the support that needs to be provided by a generic data cleaning platform for the task of *deduplication*. As motivated in Chapter 1, the goal of deduplication is to combine records that represent the same real-world entity.

Deduplication can be loosely thought of as a fuzzy or approximate variant of the relational select distinct operation. It has as its input a table and a set of columns; the output is a partition of this table where each individual group denotes a set of records that are approximately equal on the specified columns. Consider the following example showing a table containing information about people and a partition defined over all the textual columns, illustrating the output of deduplication. The first three rows in the table form one group while the last two rows form another group.

Example 8.1

Table 8.1: Table showing records with {g11, g12, g13} being one group of duplications, and {g21, g22} another set of duplicate records

ID	Name	Country
g11	Roger Federrer	Switzerland
g12	R. Federer	Switzerland
g13	Roger Federer	Swiss
g21	Novak Djokovic	Serbia
g22	Novak Jokovic	Serbia

Formally, the grouping process in deduplication can be defined as follows.

Definition 8.2 deduplication. Given a relation $R(ID, A_1, \ldots, A_n)$, construct a partitioning $\delta(R) = \{G_1, \ldots, D_m\}$ of the IDs in R, such that: (1) $\pi_{ID}(R) = \cup_{i=1..m} G_i$, (2) $\forall 1 \leq i < j \leq m : (G_i \cap G_j) = \emptyset$. Intuitively, $\forall r_1, r_2 \in R, r_1.ID, r_2.ID \in G_i$ iff r_1 and r_2 represent the same real-world entity.

Deduplication poses similar challenges as that of record matching: (1) Given a pair of records $r_1, r_2 \in R$, how do I decide whether to place them in the same group? As with record matching, this process is generally guided by a similarity measure $sim(r_1, r_2) \in [0, 1]$; however, the process is more complicated here since the decision of whether to group r_1 and r_2 together depends on other records. (2) Since R may be very large, we cannot always compare all pairs of records.

A large amount of information can be brought to bear in order to perform deduplication, namely the textual similarity between records, constraints that are expected to hold over clean data such as functional dependencies and attribute correlations that are known to exist.

We start by addressing the first challenge above. In Section 8.1, we discuss an overall graph-based approach for solving the deduplication problem. Then, in Section 8.2, we discuss the merging of grouped records to obtain the deduplication output. In Section 8.3, we discuss a common technique of guiding the deduplication process by providing external domain-specific constraints. Finally, in Section 8.4 we discuss a pre-processing technique called *blocking*, used to partition the graph into smaller groups from very large input relations, such that each group can be independently deduced. We conclude with a brief bibliography in Section 8.5.

8.1 GRAPH PARTITIONING APPROACH

We now describe a sequence of steps used to convert the deduplication problem into a graph clustering problem. Specifically, we shall convert the grouping problem from Definition 8.2 to a graph partitioning problem. The key ingredients of the constructed graph are described in the definition below:

Definition 8.3 Deduplication. Given an input instance of deduplication defined by the relation $R(ID, A_1, \ldots, A_n)$, we construct a weighted graph $G(V, E, W)$, where:

- V is the set of nodes, where each node represents a unique tuple in R
- $E \subseteq V \times V$ is a set of edges
- $W : E \rightarrow [0, 1]$ is a weight function assigning a weight for every edge. Intuitively, the weight on an edge (v_1, v_2) captures the similarity between the tuples corresponding to the nodes v_1 and v_2.

Clearly, any partitioning of the graph G corresponds to a particular deduplication output: each partition defines a group in Definition 8.3. Conversely, every deduplication output can be modeled as a partition in G above. Therefore, we can reduce the deduplication problem to—(1) construction of G, (2) partitioning of G—which are discussed next.

In Section 8.1.1, we look at computing a similarity between a given pair of records, which is at the heart of the graph construction. Then, in Section 8.1.2, we describe how the constructed graph is partitioned to obtain a grouping of records.

8.1.1 GRAPH CONSTRUCTION

At the core of the graph construction is a similarity function that measures the similarity or distance between a pair of records. It returns a similarity score which is typically a value between 0 and 1, a higher value indicating a larger similarity with 1 denoting equality. The techniques used to obtain such a similarity function are the same as that for record matching (discussed in Section 7.2.2 in Chapter 7); therefore, we don't repeat a discussion of the techniques here.

Given an input table to be deduplicated, we can apply the similarity function to all pairs of records to obtain a weighted similarity graph where the nodes are the tuples in the table and there is a weighted edge connecting each pair of nodes, the weight representing the similarity.

In practice, the complete graph is rarely computed since this involves a cross-product. Rather, only those edges whose weight is above a given threshold are materialized. As we have described in Chapter 4, we can use the similarity join operator to efficiently compute pairwise similarity scores only for pairs that meet a certain threshold.

8.1.2 GRAPH PARTITIONING

Let's call the similarity graph where only edges with weights greater than a threshold are present as the *threshold graph*. The grouping in our deduplication task is now performed by partitioning of the nodes in the threshold graph. Intuitively, we desire a partition where nodes that are connected with larger edge weights have a greater likelihood of being in the same group. Since similarity functions often do not satisfy properties such as triangle inequality, there are multiple ways of partitioning the similarity graph. We may therefore use an implementation of the clustering operator described in Chapter 5; however, we need a clustering operation that ensures a *disjoint partition*, i.e., each node is in exactly one output cluster. Typical partitioning approaches for deduplication either consider connected components (often called the *single linkage partitioning*) of the threshold graph, or partitioning into cliques.

The above single linkage and clique partitioning approaches are applicable to several scenarios. But their applicability is restricted because the user cannot influence the result of deduplication easily, other than setting the threshold while constructing the threshold graph. Beyond that threshold and choosing one of single linkage or clique partitioning, a user cannot really influence the deduplication task in this approach. Setting thresholds and iteratively analyzing results to determine a better threshold is quite hard. In Section 8.3, we discuss other mechanisms by which users may influence the result of deduplication.

8.2 MERGING

One post-processing task of deduplication is to *merge* tuples in each group to identify or to even create a canonical tuple that represents the entire group. In other words, given group $G_i \in \delta(R)$ as defined in Definition 8.3, we need to apply a process $Merge(G_i)$ to obtain a single tuple t combining the values of attributes from each tuple in G_i.

Example 8.4 Going back to the example grouping from Example 8.1, we can combine the group $G_1 = \{g11, g12, g13\}$ to obtain a single tuple t as follows:

Table 8.2: Table showing the merged record t obtained from the group of records {g11, g12, g13} from Example 8.1

ID	Name	Country
t	Roger Federer	Switzerland

The idea behind merging is to create a single record for each real-world entity, which is challenging because of the discrepancies in the attribute values among the tuples constituting a group. At a high level, there are two approaches in dealing with merging: (1) Maintain multiple possible values for attributes if it is not clear which value is right, and leave it to downstream processing to handle the uncertainty in the values. (2) Construct a tuple with no uncertainty by obtaining the best value for each tuple, known as *conflict resolution*.

There are multiple ways in which an attribute value may be picked during the conflict resolution process. A common approach is to pick the "most likely" value among the ones that appear in the tuples. The process of determining the most likely value depends on the type of attribute, the domain, and available information. Below we give examples of cues that can be used:

- **Frequency:** If an attribute value appears more frequently among multiple input tuples, it is more likely to be correct.
- **Source Authority:** If we know that one of the input tuples is obtained from a more authoritative source database, e.g., the U.S. Census, it is more likely to contain correct values.
- **Attribute Domain:** We can use domains of attributes (e.g., $age \in [0, 100]$) to weed out incorrect values.

Also note that in order to compare values across tuples, we may first need to convert all of them into the same type (e.g., convert all temperatures to Fahrenheit). In more complicated scenarios, we may construct a new attribute value that didn't appear in any input tuple. For example, if one tuple only had the first name and another tuple had the last name in a "Name" attribute, we would like to concatenate them to construct the full name. In our example above, the output name is "Sweet legal Investments Incorporated," which is obtained by correcting the spelling of investments in the input tuple. Therefore, this output value is not present in any input tuple.

8.3 USING CONSTRAINTS FOR DEDUPLICATION

Beyond clustering and partitioning approaches for splitting a graph, deduplication can be further guided by constraints on the groups resulting from partitioning. We now discuss a few examples and types of constraints that are commonly considered for deduplication.

- Constraints on individual tuples: These are constraints that express the condition that only some tuples (for instance "products that have sold in December") may participate in the deduplication. Such constraints are easily enforced by pushing these filter conditions before deduplication is invoked.

- Deduplication parameters as constraints: Several deduplication algorithms take parameters such as the number of groups to be output as constraints. The idea here is roughly similar to clustering in that a user may know the "approximate" number of unique records in a relation. This knowledge can be leveraged for deduplication.

- Pairwise positive and negative examples: These are constraints that require some pairs of tuples be grouped together and that other pairs not be grouped together. Such example pairs can be often be obtained either while browsing a sample of records in a relation or while reviewing preliminary results from deduplication.

- Groupwise constraints: These are constraints that are required to be satisfied by each group in the output of deduplication. These constraints are often based on the domain expertise. For example, the total amount billed to all customer records being grouped together must equal the total amount of goods shipped for each of them.

Our goal now is to incorporate these constraints along with the similarity function, and achieve the best possible deduplication solution. Satisfying all constraints may not always be possible. In fact, even determining whether or not all constraints are satisfiable is NP-hard. So, the typical approach has been to satisfy as many constraints as possible, over a "candidate set" of partitions.

The separation of the candidate set of partitions from the algorithm for choosing the best partition enables us to incorporate domain-specific constraints. In some scenarios, it is possible to consider connected components as candidate groups. That is, nodes which are connected (indirectly through any chain of neighbors) may be considered duplicates. While in some other scenarios, it is required that all nodes in a group must be connected directly. Separating the definition of a candidate set of partitions from the choice of the best partition enables this framework to achieve both solutions, and the developer has to specify the desired one. We now discuss candidate sets of partitions and then using the constraints to identify the best partition from among the candidate set.

8.3.1 CANDIDATE SETS OF PARTITIONS

We now discuss restricting the sets of candidate sets of groupings. The restriction enables us to effectively use constraints and to efficiently find the right deduplication solution.

We describe this candidate space procedurally as follows. Note that this procedure is not actually executed but only used to define the candidate sets of partitions. We begin with a coarse initial partition of the tuples in R. Logically, we assume all tuples in R to be collapsed into one group. We then split the individual groups by examining the similarity graph induced over the tuples in the group and deleting low weight edges until the graph gets disconnected. The new connected components define the split of the original group. We iterate in this manner with each of the split groups till we are left with singleton groups.

Formally, we define the space of valid groups as follows. Given a group of tuples, its *splitting threshold* is the lowest value of similarity α such that thresholding the similarity graph (induced over the group) at α disconnects it. The split of a group of tuples is the resulting set of connected components. We recurse on each individual component until each tuple forms its own group. This procedure defines the set of all valid groups and is not actually executed.

We can procedurally define the space of valid groups as follows:

- Initialize the set of valid groups with the groups in a seed partition.
- For each group, add its *split* to the set.
- Recurse until we cannot add new groups.

8.3.2 MAXIMIZING CONSTRAINT SATISFACTION

The goal now is to identify the best partition from among the candidate set of partitions. We now describe the algorithm for choosing the "best" set of groups that satisfy the given set of constraints. First, we have to define the notion of *benefit*, which quantifies the quality of a partition.

Definition 8.5 The *benefit* of a partition is the number of groups that satisfy all constraints.

Other notions of benefit such as the sum of the number of records in all groups which satisfy constraints may also be considered in this framework.

Informally, the algorithm proceeds as follows. We first start with a seed partition (which can be the entire relation), and then recursively split each group in the partition until the benefit continues to improve. At any point, the current stage of the algorithm defines a *frontier*, which is being expanded. Note that each group in the current frontier can be independently split further without considering its impact on the rest of the groups. This independence allows us to efficiently arrive at a desirable partition that maximizes the benefit. So, a developer can solely focus on setting up the constraints that model an ideal deduplication of the given dataset.

8.4 BLOCKING

Since the input relation to be deduplicated may be very large, a pairwise comparison of all records is often infeasible. To get around this problem, a process known as *blocking* is typically applied. Blocking performs a coarser granularity clustering of R such that we only need to compare records within each cluster for the final clustering.

Definition 8.6 **Blocking.** Given a relation $R(ID, A_1, \ldots, A_n)$, construct a *blocking* $\mathcal{B} = \{B_1, \ldots, B_m\}$ such that: (1) $\forall i : B_i \subseteq R$; (2) $\delta(R) \approx \cup_{i=1..m}\delta(B_i)$.

One commonly used blocking technique is to perform *hashing* of records based on attributes, thereby resulting in *disjoint* blocks. In some cases, we may want to hash on multiple attributes, leading to *non-disjoint* blocks, in which case groupings from each of the block may need further processing (rather than just the union as described in Definition 8.6) to ensure that each tuple in R is eventually place in only one group.

8.5 BIBLIOGRAPHY

Christen [2012a] is a generic study of deduplication. Arasu et al. [2009], Chaudhuri et al. [2007], Guo et al. [2010], and Fan et al. [2011] have studied constraint-based deduplication; each of these contain additional references on deduplication. Christen [2012b] surveys blocking, and Bilenko et al. [2006], Michelson and Knoblock [2006], and Das Sarma et al. [2012] study in detail automated blocking techniques. Sarawagi and Bhamidipaty [2002] study interactive deduplication.

CHAPTER 9

Data Cleaning Scripts

The operator-centric approach for data cleaning enables customized development of efficient and accurate solutions to data cleaning tasks relatively easily. The heavy lifting is expected to be done by the core operators while the custom solution may leverage operations such as standard relational operators as well as other predicates, which are required for the specific data and domain being considered. Thus, the development of custom data cleaning scripts is expected to be flexible, easy, and efficient all at the same time.

In this chapter, we will discuss the development of custom data cleaning solutions based on data cleaning operators discussed in the previous chapters. These solutions can be viewed as "scripts" involving the operators, or as plans in the traditional query processing representation. Our goal is to illustrate the richness of the operator-based approach in developing customized data cleaning solutions. We consider the record matching and deduplication tasks to illustrate this.

9.1 RECORD MATCHING SCRIPTS

Recall that the goal of record matching is to identify pairs of records across two relations that identify the same real world entity. This is particularly useful while inserting new records into an existing relation, say customers, or when matching product offers from merchants with a master catalog of products.

Let us consider two input customer relations. Let C1's schema be (Id, Name, Address, City, State, Zip, Gender) and C2's schema be (Id, First Name, Middle Initial, Last Name, Address, Gender). In the case when C1.Id and C2.Id are from the same domain then a sample script for matching C1 and C2 is shown in Figure 9.1. We first rely on the Ids matching to find matching record pairs. We then also join records based on a similarity measure over the concatenation of Name and Address columns in order to identify closely matching records. However, note that the first and last names are in separate columns in C2 while they are concatenated together in C1. So, we first concatenate the two columns before performing a similarity join. Also, notice that the join for identifying matches has multiple join predicates: equality join on the City and Zip columns followed by a similarity join on the Name and Address columns.

In the scenario when C1 and C2 are captured by two different databases, then matching on Id may be meaningless. In this scenario, we cannot rely on individual attribute address attribute values being specified correctly in all records. Therefore, we primarily rely on the textual similarity and use the SSJoin operator to identify such pairs. We then ensure that only pairs whose gender values are equal are considered to match. We illustrate the script in Figure 9.2.

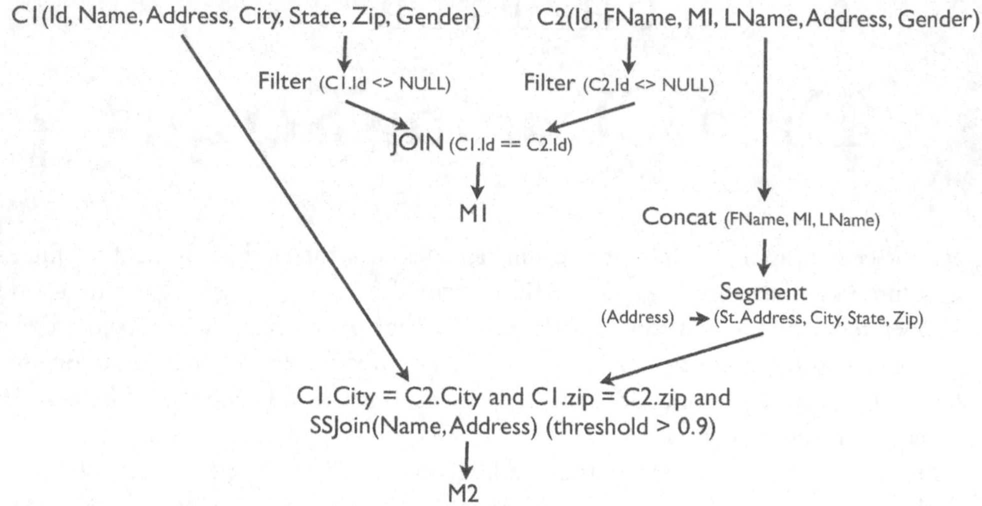

Figure 9.1: Record matching: Example script 1.

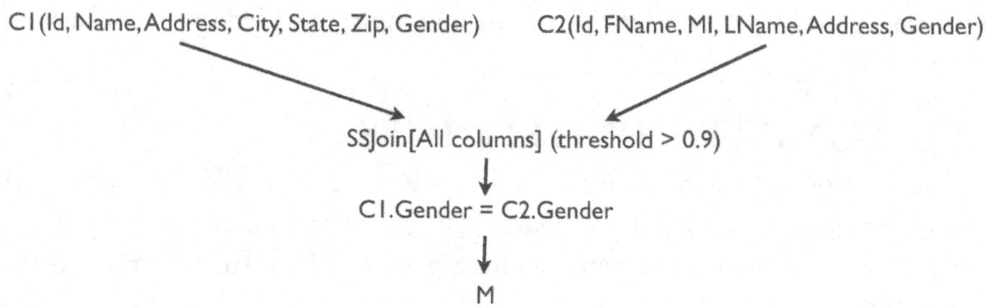

Figure 9.2: Record matching: Example Script 2.

The flexibility of preparing an execution plan that suits the specific scenario is illustrated by the above scripts trying to solve the same record matching task between two given relations. The script can be targeted toward the scenario and the characteristics of the data thus allowing a lot of flexibility and ability to comprehensively address the problem.

9.2 DEDUPLICATION SCRIPTS

Recall that the goal of deduplication is to group records in a relation such that each group represents the same real-world entity. This operation is useful when merging multiple customer databases into a single master customer repository. A similar task arises when merging product catalogs from multiple sources into a single master product catalog.

Let us consider an input relation of customer records with schema (Id, Name, Address, City, State, Zip, Gender). The task of deduping customer records in this relation could be approached through one of two scripts shown in Figures 9.3 and 9.4, respectively.

In the first script, we materialize the similarity graph and then apply a constrained clustering in order to deduplicate customer records. We compare pairs of records in C based on the Name, Address, City, State, Zip, and Gender values to construct a similarity graph with edges between records with a high similarity. We then apply constraints based on the domain. Suppose we know that each customer may be replicated in at most 10 records. And suppose we anticipate the gender value is usually recorded accurately and hence most of the records in a group must share the dominant value. Then, we may stipulate the constraints shown in Figure 9.3. The output of the script is a solution for the deduplication task.

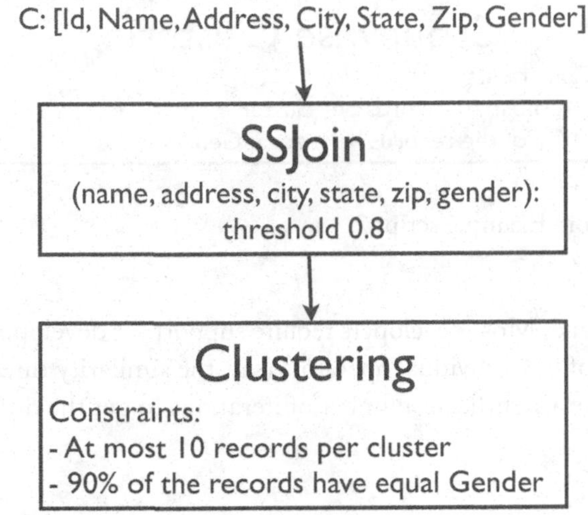

Figure 9.3: Deduplication: Example script 1.

In a different scenario, suppose we knew based on the specific scenario that gender and zip values in individual records are almost always correctly recorded, we can then approach the deduplication task as follows (also depicted in Figure 9.4). We first group records based on Gender and Zip values. We then apply constraint-based clustering within each group to identify records describing the same entity. This script better leverages the domain knowledge to be more efficient and potentially more accurate as well. Once again, like in the case for record matching, these scripts illustrate the power and flexibility of the operator-centric approach.

9.3 SUPPORT FOR SCRIPT DEVELOPMENT

Even though allowing the development of scripts in order to achieve a data cleaning task is fairly general, the actual development of such scripts requires significant domain expertise and knowl-

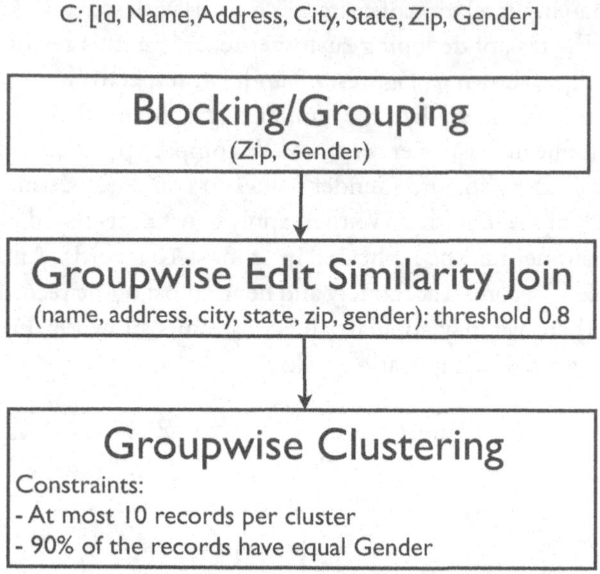

Figure 9.4: Deduplication: Example script 2.

edge of the data set at hand. Most developers require support for developing such scripts. Further, even configuring some of the individual operators (say, the similarity threshold in the SSJoin operator) could also involve a significant number of iterations to get the desired output quality, and even efficiency.

9.3.1 USER INTERFACE FOR DEVELOPING SCRIPTS

Providing a great user interface where developers can easily write efficient and accurate data cleaning scripts with support for an extensive operator palette—including both pre-defined operators such as data cleaning operators and standard relational operators—is critical. Further, this environment should allow users to define their own custom transformation operators so as to be effective. The language in which custom operators are developed and registered with the palette is important as well—choice that is popular among developers would be make the palette much more compelling.

The interface could provide a graphical view of the resulting data flow. The graphical view enables a developer to quickly get an overview of the data flow. Based on this view, they would be able to easily adjust the data flow by either adding or modifying existing operators, or by re-wiring the flow. Once the data flow is designed, the user interface must allow a developer to test the script based on a small sample dataset. They can use these test runs to validate their assumptions on the data that their script is going to process. This functionality allows developers to fix errors in the script—both in the wiring of the operators as well as in the custom scripts they may have developed.

Interactive data transformation environments for developing custom transformation scripts and reusing scripts written by previous users would be tremendously useful. The transformation scripts could involve a variety of operations including common relational operators such as joins and a few important enhancements such as the following: (i) Splitting a string into attribute values based on regular expressions or learning examples, as done by the parsing operator discussed earlier. (ii) Extracting sub-strings from strings as attribute values; this is a generalization of the parsing operator. (iii) Pivot and unpivot operators, which transform the structure of the data. The interactive user interface allows users to combine these operators to develop scripts that transform the input data as required.

9.3.2 CONFIGURABLE DATA CLEANING SCRIPTS

One approach is to identify the most common domains and data characteristics and prepare custom scripts. Let us consider the popular domain of U.S. addresses. We could develop a *templatized configurable script* for cleaning of data consisting of U.S. addresses. We refer to this as a templatized script because the script must still be configurable to satisfy the requirements of the specific dataset and application in consideration. Further, the custom script must include support for all standard data cleaning tasks such as record matching, deduplication, and parsing. For example, it must be possible to adjust the thresholds of similarity joins or other constraints that are typical of a deduplication task. An application which is trying to identify ten thousand addresses to mail a catalog would require a different configuration of constraints than an application which is attempting to comprehensively group all unique addresses. Therefore, these custom data cleaning scripts must be enable such configuration.

In general, domains which are encountered across several applications and enterprises could benefit from this approach. Once a comprehensive set of scripts are developed they can now be used across many enterprises and applications. The domain of U.S. addresses has the potential, since most enterprises in the U.S. would encounter this problem, and can benefit from these scripts. The domain of electronics or other categories of products is another popular one which could lend itself to adoption of configurable data cleaning scripts.

Note that the implementation of these scripts may internally leverage the operator-centric approach. The scripts could exploit the knowledge of the domain they are intended to work for, and rely on all these operators to develop the operator flow. And they would expose a limited set of configurable parameters that are meaningful for the specific domain of choice.

A complementary approach to further help users choose the correct configuration parameters for a specific dataset is to leverage an example-based machine learning approach. A typical approach here is to get users to label a set of input records and the expected output—depending on the data cleaning task being considered—for the specific dataset. Based on the labels, learn the parameters that would achieve the best accuracy as per the examples. This is a non-trivial problem and there are many open technical challenges which need to be addressed in implementing this approach accurately and robustly. How many examples would be required to learn the parameters fairly accurately? How would the approaches deal with a small fraction of errors in the labeled examples? These are a few of the technical challenges which need to be addressed for each data cleaning task.

9.4 BIBLIOGRAPHY

Many commercial ETL engines enable the development of graphs of operators—including predefined and custom operators. Examples of such commercial ETL engines include IBM Ascential and SSIS. Many research prototypes have also proposed platforms for creating and executing data flow scripts to develop custom solutions—transforming data to populate data warehouses as well as to clean it [Chaudhuri et al., 2006a, Dohzen et al., 2006, Galhardas et al., 2000]. At the same time, tools to help the creation of such data flow scripts over these platforms for specific data cleaning tasks are also being developed. Many interactive tools for developing and reusing data transformation scripts based on a rich set of operators have been developed [Kandel et al., 2011, Raman and Hellerstein, 2001].

CHAPTER 10

Conclusion

We discussed various aspects of data cleaning technology, including its goals, approaches to implementing effective solutions, and several critical components of the technology. The goals of data cleaning technology in typical enterprise scenarios, as illustrated by the examples in customer and product databases, are to maintain the quality and consistency of data as the data warehouse is either being populated with data for the first time or being updated with fresh data subsequently. These solutions are typically incorporated into an ETL process which is maintained in order to populate and maintain a data warehouse. A data cleaning solution is expected to address to several critical high level tasks. Some of these tasks include *record matching*, *deduplication*, and *parsing*.

The goal of record matching is to efficiently and accurately match pairs of records across relations for evaluating whether or not they are semantically equivalent. The task could be customized (by developers or custom applications) to use specific similarity functions or filters in conjunction with a similarity function. The record matching task could be applied to check for duplicates in an incoming batch of new customer or product records to avoid insertion of duplicate entities into the data warehouse.

The goal of deduplication is to efficiently group records in a relation where each group of records represent the same real-world entity. A developer of a deduplication task must be able to influence the grouping to satisfy some expected constraints such as those between known pairs of records or on the properties of the groups of records. The deduplication task could be applied to merge multiple records representing the same logical entity. Such a merge will improve the quality of downstream reporting.

The goal of the parsing task is to extract attribute values from an input record or string before inserting them into the target relation, say customer or product. Often, input records are pulled from an external source system and hence the formats could be very different. The parsing task is critical to transform an input record or string from such a system into the target system's structure.

A few common approaches are usually adopted for solving these data cleaning tasks: (i) domain-specific solutions which are customized to specific domains, (ii) generic platforms which are very general but require the developer to do most of the work by implementing the logic behind a data cleaning task, and (iii) an operator-based approach which provide generic operators using which customized solutions for data cleaning tasks may be implemented.

We then discussed the operator-based approach and described several critical data cleaning operators—set similarity join, clustering, and parsing. The set similarity join operator efficiently matches pairs of records between relations and could be used to efficiently implement the similarity join between relations using a variety of similarity functions. Hence, a developer can easily build on top of the set similarity join to implement an efficient and accurate solution for the record matching task. The clustering operator groups records in a relation and allows developers to incorporate a rich class of constraints each group in the output or a collection of output groups has to respect. Hence, developers can build on top of the clustering operator to implement an efficient and accurate solution for the deduplication task. The parsing operator allows a developer to specify regular expressions or examples to illustrate the parsing of an input record into the target structure. Hence, it may be used to implement an efficient and custom solution for the parsing task.

All of the above critical data cleaning operators can be used with standard relational operators as well as other custom operators to develop efficient and accurate data cleaning technology. We illustrated the flexibility of the operator-based approach with several example scripts to implement record matching and deduplication tasks.

There are several technical issues that we have not discussed. For instance, we haven't discussed the integration of these operators or custom tasks into an ETL platform. We also have skipped the discussion of some relevant technologies such as information extraction, which is useful for extracting attribute values from strings, and schema mapping which is useful for ensuring that the schema and semantics of columns across data sources are the same. We have also skipped issues such as learning-based techniques for developing scripts. It is often easier for developers to provide examples of desired output and we can bring to bear several machine learning technologies to help with the intermediate development of scripts. Another issue that we have not discussed is that of collaboration among developers working with the same dataset in order to develop effective data cleaning scripts. Often, developers often rewrite transformations and scripts that people have already developed before. Developing tools which enable effective collaboration on data transformation and data cleaning scripts is an active area of engineering and research.

In summary, we have provided a biased overview of the various problems, approaches, and techniques that have been developed in the context of data cleaning. We anticipate that this area of data cleaning will continue to evolve over the next several years, both in the research and in the commercial domains.

Bibliography

Arvind Arasu, Venkatesh Ganti, and Raghav Kaushik. Efficient exact set-similarity joins. In *Proc. 32nd Int. Conf. on Very Large Data Bases*, pages 918–929, 2006. 28

Arvind Arasu, Christopher Ré, and Dan Suciu. Large-scale deduplication with constraints using dedupalog. In *Proc. 25th Int. Conf. on Data Engineering*, pages 952–963, 2009. DOI: 10.1109/ICDE.2009.43. 55

Roberto J. Bayardo, Yiming Ma, and Ramakrishnan Srikant. Scaling up all pairs similarity search. In *Proc. 16th Int. World Wide Web Conf.*, pages 131–140, 2007. DOI: 10.1145/1242572.1242591. 28

Mikhail Bilenko, Beena Kamath, and Raymond J. Mooney. Adaptive blocking: Learning to scale up record linkage and clustering. In *Proc. 2006 IEEE Int. Conf. on Data Mining*, pages 87–96, 2006. DOI: 10.1109/ICDM.2006.13. 55

Vinayak Borkar, Kaustubh Deshmukh, and Sunita Sarawagi. Automatic segmentation of text into structured records. In *Proc. ACM SIGMOD Int. Conf. on Management of Data*, pages 175–186, May 2001. DOI: 10.1145/376284.375682. 42

Mary Elaine Califf and Raymond J. Mooney. Relational learning of pattern-match rules for information extraction. In *Proc. 16th National Conf. on Artificial Intelligence and 11th Innovative Applications of Artificial Intelligence Conf.*, pages 328–334, 1999. 42

Surajit Chaudhuri, Venkatesh Ganti, and Raghav Kaushik. Data debugger: An operator-centric approach for data quality solutions. *Q. Bull. IEEE TC on Data Eng.*, 29(2):60–66, 2006a. 11, 62

Surajit Chaudhuri, Venkatesh Ganti, and Raghav Kaushik. A primitive operator for similarity joins in data cleaning. In *Proc. 22nd Int. Conf. on Data Engineering*, 2006b. DOI: 10.1109/ICDE.2006.9. 28

Surajit Chaudhuri, Anish Das Sarma, Venkatesh Ganti, and Raghav Kaushik. Leveraging aggregate constraints for deduplication. In *Proc. ACM SIGMOD Int. Conf. on Management of Data*, pages 437–448, 2007. DOI: 10.1145/1247480.1247530. 55

Laura Chiticariu, Rajasekar Krishnamurthy, Yunyao Li, Sriram Raghavan, Frederick Reiss, and Shivakumar Vaithyanathan. SystemT: An algebraic approach to declarative information extraction. In *Proc. 48th Annual Meeting Assoc. for Computational Linguistics*, pages 128–137, 2010. 42

Peter Christen. *Data Matching - Concepts and Techniques for Record Linkage, Entity Resolution, and Duplicate Detection*. Springer, 2012a. DOI: 10.1007/978-3-642-31164-2. 48, 55

Peter Christen. A survey of indexing techniques for scalable record linkage and deduplication. *IEEE Trans. Knowl. and Data Eng.*, 24(9):1537–1555, 2012b. DOI: 10.1109/TKDE.2011.127. 55

W. Cohen, P. Ravikumar, and S. E. Fienberg. A Comparison of String Distance Metrics for Name-Matching Tasks. In *Proc. 18th Int. Joint Conf. on AI*, pages 73–78, 2003. 16, 48

Anish Das Sarma, Ankur Jain, Ashwin Machanavajjhala, and Philip Bohannon. An automatic blocking mechanism for large-scale de-duplication tasks. In *Proc. 21st ACM Int. Conf. on Information and Knowledge Management*, pages 1055–1064, 2012. DOI: 10.1145/2396761.2398403. 34, 55

Tiffany Dohzen, Mujde Pamuk, Seok-Won Seong, Joachim Hammer, and Michael Stonebraker. Data integration through transform reuse in the morpheus project. In *Proc. ACM SIGMOD Int. Conf. on Management of Data*, pages 736–738, 2006. DOI: 10.1145/1142473.1142571. 11, 62

Wenfei Fan, Hong Gao, Xibei Jia, Jianzhong Li, and Shuai Ma. Dynamic constraints for record matching. *VLDB J.*, 20(4):495–520, 2011. DOI: 10.1007/s00778-010-0206-6. 55

I. P. Fellegi and A. B. Sunter. A theory for record linkage. *J. American Statistical Soc.*, 64(328): 1183–1210, 1969. DOI: 10.1080/01621459.1969.10501049. 48

Helena Galhardas, Daniela Florescu, Dennis Shasha, and Eric Simon. An extensible framework for data cleaning. In *Proc. 16th Int. Conf. on Data Engineering*, pages 312–312, 2000. DOI: 10.1109/ICDE.2000.839429. 11, 62

Luis Gravano, Panagiotis G. Ipeirotis, H. V. Jagadish, Nick Koudas, S. Muthukrishnan, and Divesh Srivastava. Approximate string joins in a database (almost) for free. In *Proc. 27th Int. Conf. on Very Large Data Bases*, pages 491–500, 2001. 28

Songtao Guo, Xin Luna Dong, Divesh Srivastava, and Remi Zajac. Record linkage with uniqueness constraints and erroneous values. *Proc. VLDB Endowment*, 3(1–2), 2010. 55

Jiawei Han and Micheline Kamber. *Data mining: concepts and techniques*. Morgan Kaufmann, 2006. 34

Sean Kandel, Andreas Paepcke, Joseph Hellerstein, and Jeffrey Heer. Wrangler: interactive visual specification of data transformation scripts. In *Proc. SIGCHI Conf. on Human Factors in Computing Systems*, pages 3363–3372, 2011. DOI: 10.1145/1978942.1979444. 62

Nick Koudas, Sunita Sarawagi, and Divesh Srivastava. Record linkage: Similarity measures and algorithms. Tutorial at SIGMOD Conference, 2006. 16, 28, 48

Andrew Mccallum and Dayne Freitag. Maximum entropy markov models for information extraction and segmentation. In *Proc. 17th Int. Conf. on Machine Learning*, pages 591–598, 2000. 42

Matthew Michelson and Craig A. Knoblock. Learning blocking schemes for record linkage. In *Proc. 21st National Conf. on Artificial Intelligence and 18th Innovative Applications of Artificial Intelligence Conf.*, pages 440–445, 2006. 55

H. B. Newcombe, J. M. Kennedy, S. J. Axford, and A. P. James. Automatic linkage of vital records. *Science*, 130(3381):954–959, 1959. DOI: 10.1126/science.130.3381.954. 48

Vijayshankar Raman and Joe Hellerstein. Potter's wheel: An interactive data cleaning system. In *Proc. 27th Int. Conf. on Very Large Data Bases*, pages 381–390, 2001. 62

Sunita Sarawagi and Anuradha Bhamidipaty. Interactive deduplication using active learning. In *Proc. 8th ACM SIGKDD Int. Conf. on Knowledge Discovery and Data Mining*, pages 269–278, 2002. DOI: 10.1145/775047.775087. 55

Sunita Sarawagi and William W. Cohen. Semi-markov conditional random fields for information extraction. In *Advances in Neural Information Processing Systems 17*, pages 1185–1192, 2004. 42

Sunita Sarawagi and Alok Kirpal. Efficient set joins on similarity predicates. In *Proc. ACM SIGMOD Int. Conf. on Management of Data*, pages 743–754, 2004. DOI: 10.1145/1007568.1007652. 28

Rares Vernica, Michael J. Carey, and Chen Li. Efficient parallel set-similarity joins using mapreduce. In *Proc. ACM SIGMOD Int. Conf. on Management of Data*, pages 495–506, 2010. DOI: 10.1145/1807167.1807222. 28

Chuan Xiao, Wei Wang, and Xuemin Lin. Ed-join: an efficient algorithm for similarity joins with edit distance constraints. *Proc. VLDB Endowment*, 1(1):933–944, 2008. 28

Authors' Biographies

VENKATESH GANTI

Venky Ganti is the co-founder and CTO of Alation Inc, where he is developing technology to effectively search, understand, and analyze structured and semi-structured data. Prior to Alation, he was a member of the Google Adwords engineering team for a few years. He helped develop the Dynamic Search Ads (DSA) product, whose goal is to completely automate the configuration and maintenance of AdWords campaigns based on an advertiser's website and a few configuration parameters. The main technical challenge is to mine for appropriate keywords and automatically create high quality ads which match the accuracy and quality of manually configured campaigns. Prior to Google, Venky was a senior researcher at Microsoft Research (MSR). While at MSR, he worked extensively on data cleaning and integration technologies. Some of the technologies he helped develop in this context are now part of Microsoft SQL Server Integration Services, the ETL platform of Microsoft SQL Server. He also worked on leveraging rich structured databases on products, movies, people, etc., to enrich user experience for web search. Some of the technologies he helped develop are now part of the Bing product search. He has a Ph.D. in database systems and data mining from the University of Wisconsin-Madison.

ANISH DAS SARMA

Anish Das Sarma is currently a Senior Research Scientist at Google (since May 2010), before which he was a Research Scientist at Yahoo (August 2009–April 2010). Prior to joining Yahoo research, Anish did his Ph.D. in Computer Science at Stanford University, advised by Prof. Jennifer Widom. Anish received a B.Tech. in Computer Science and Engineering from the Indian Institute of Technology (IIT) Bombay in 2004, and an M.S. in Computer Science from Stanford University in 2006. Anish is a recipient of the Microsoft Graduate Fellowship, a Stanford University School of Engineering fellowship, and the IIT-Bombay Dr. Shankar Dayal Sharma Gold Medal. Anish has written over 40 technical papers, filed over 10 patents, is associate editor of *Sigmod Record*, has served on the thesis committee of a Stanford Ph.D. student, and has served on numerous program committees. Two SIGMOD and one VLDB paper co-authored by Anish were selected among the best papers of the conference, with invitations to journals. While at Stanford, Anish co-founded Shout Velocity, a social tweet ranking system that was named a top-50 fbFund Finalist for most promising upcoming start-up ideas.

Printed in the United States
by Baker & Taylor Publisher Services